Pumpkins & Squashes

Recipes, propagation and decoration

Janet Macdonald

Grub Street • London

For Vincent and Angela, and all my other squash-loving friends

First published in 1998 by
Grub Street
The Basement
10 Chivalry Road
London SW11 1HT

British Library Cataloguing in Publication Data for this title is available from the British
Library

ISBN 1 898697 71 X

Jacket and book design by
Adam Denchfield Design

Printed and bound in Italy by
Vallardi Industrie Grafiche SpA

Contents

Introduction

I first encountered squash on a visit to Canada. The friends we stayed with served a dish heaped up with mashed Buttercup squash, golden, fluffy and delicious. I'd never tasted anything like it and enthused so much that they gave me some seeds to bring home, and I've been growing my own squash ever since.

That was over ten years ago, and at that time you couldn't buy seeds of anything but basic pumpkin here, let alone the fruits of this wonderful vegetable. Now you find squash in most supermarkets, and several seed companies offer a good variety of both pumpkins and squash, and their close relatives, courgettes.

Despite this, recipe books offer little besides Pumpkin Pie, Squash Soup or Risotto. Whenever I mention squash, people say "Oh yes, I've seen them but I don't know what to do with them," - but I know from my travels and my own experiments that there isn't much you can't do with them! We've been eating them in gratins, stews, sweet and savoury pies, ice-cream, and in many other forms.

As well as being a versatile food, squash is good for you. The flesh of all the squash family is full of vitamins A and C. Summer squash, including courgettes, are high in niacin; and winter squash and pumpkins contain iron, potassium and zinc, as well as the anti-oxidants beta-carotene and vitamin E. The seeds, or the salad oil made from them, are also rich in vitamins and anti-oxidants, and have traditionally been used in folk medicine to prevent cancer, reduce prostate inflammation and expel intestinal worms.

But for me, the main reason for eating anything is that it tastes good, and these wonderful vegetables certainly fill that criterion. I decided it was time to share my collection of recipes with a wider audience than my immediate circle of friends. I won't say that I've included every possible way to cook squash, but I think I've covered most of them.

I hope that after you've tried some of them for yourself, you'll share my enthusiasm.

Janet Macdonald

A Little History

Pumpkins and squashes, and their close relatives, gourds, have an ancient history - evidence has been found of their use almost 10,000 years ago. Gourds, with shapes ranging from more or less spherical to bottle-shaped, are still hollowed out and used as storage pots for grains, nuts or liquids (not to mention penis protectors, although where the larger gourds are used, one wonders if a certain amount of boasting is involved.)

They make spoons, and scooping implements. I still use a half-calabash which was given to me by a Guyanan neighbour when I lived in a flat with an enormous cast-iron bath but no method of heating enough water to fill it. With a bucket full of hot water, I could stand in the bath and scoop calabashfuls of water over myself - a very effective way of 'showering'. It gets used for hair-washing now, but I'm still very grateful to Joyce for the gift.

They have been, and still are used as cricket cages, breeding boxes for canaries, pipes for tobacco and (whisper it) marijuana, fishing floats, ceremonial masks, and all sorts of musical instruments, from maracas and drums to flutes for snake charming.

Gourds (*Lagenaria*) evolved throughout the tropical world, but the edible summer and winter squashes and pumpkins are New World natives, originating from South and Central America. You occasionally come across a writer who states that pumpkins were used by the Romans, but this is an error due to the fact that the word pumpkin is derived via the 17th Century word *pompion* from the Greek word for melon - *pepon*, which was also used by Romans.

Brought by European explorers from the Americas, where they are traditionally eaten mainly in soups and stews (and where the seeds were used as a tasty way of getting rid of intestinal worms), they became incorporated into the cooking of their new homes. In Italy pumpkins are used in risotto or to stuff pasta, in France the courgette was traditionally preferred, in England it was the mature version of courgette, the marrow, that caught the gardener's imagination.

European settlers in North America were given pumpkins by the native Americans, together with other local foods including turkeys and cranberries. Their gratitude for these gifts, which helped them survive their first year, is celebrated each November in the traditional Thanksgiving dinner of roast turkey and pumpkin pie.

Americans have, for many years, also enjoyed the more complex taste of the winter squashes, but it is only in the last few years that these have been freely available in Europe. In France, pumpkins used to be thought of as cattle food, but they, and winter squashes, are enjoying a surge of popularity.

There are regular pumpkin fairs throughout France during the autumn (for dates and locations, see page 166) where you can see, taste, and buy, all the types of squash, pumpkin and gourds, and also try your skill at such arcane arts as long distance pip spitting. Artists visit these fairs to create sculptures in the style of Archimbaldo, display paintings of squash and pumpkins, or just sell carved and painted gourds. As well as squash and pumpkins, you can see and buy many other ancient and rare vegetables and fruit.

Few people realise that the fairy story 'Cinderella' originated in France, where the heroine is called Cendrillon. Quite what made someone first think that a pumpkin could be used as a coach I don't know, although anyone who has grown a big pumpkin is aware of the almost magical way it expands from day to day. I've always loved that story, and when I acquired my first Mercedes car (a very old one, and quite cheap) I called it Pumpkin as a propitiation to the gods, in case it turned into a pumpkin overnight. I've had a sequence of them since, and they've all been called Pumpkin. It obviously works, because none of them has turned back, even if I am out in them after midnight!

Definitions

I am often asked "What's the difference between a pumpkin and a squash?"

Unfortunately there isn't a simple answer. If you want the strictly scientific answer, it is that all are members of the *Cucurbita* family, which is split up into roughly seven types. Three of these are in common cultivation:

- *C. pepo* - this type is thought to have originated in Mexico, and includes most of the smaller winter squash such as Acorn or Golden Delicious and all the summer squash.
- *C. moschata* - this type is thought to have originated in Central America and includes some of the pumpkin varieties and some winter squash.
- *C. maxima* - this type originated in an area of South America which covers Peru, Chile, Bolivia, Paraguay and Northern Argentina. It includes both pumpkins and winter squash.

The main way to tell the difference is by the stem of the fruit, but even this is not fool-proof. In general, though, the stem of *C. pepo* and *C. moschata* are angular, with five distinct sides, while the stem of *C. maxima* is round.

The problem is that all the *Cucurbita* family are extremely promiscuous and will cross-breed with other branches of the family. This has proved beneficial when resulting in the tremendous variety of types and cultivars, but not when trying to give a simple answer to the question we started with.

Then, to add to the confusion, in some countries, (especially Australia) squash are called pumpkins and pumpkins are called squash. The only answer is to do what I do and separate them by their eating qualities. So if it is soft skinned and white fleshed, I either call it a courgette or summer squash. Pumpkins are the round jobs with delicate or bland tasting flesh, almost always orange coloured and more or less spherical (except that just to be awkward, some of the tiny ones are nearly white and the French variety Rouge Vif d'Etamps is a deep reddish-orange). Then the denser fleshed varieties with the nutty and sometimes almost sweet taste are winter squash.

If all that has got you even more confused than you were to start with, just look at the varieties detailed on pages 8-9 to see which category they are under.

Growing Your Own

Whether you grow cucumbers, courgettes, summer squash, pumpkins or winter squash, the cultivation requirements are the same. All of these members of the *Cucurbitacea* family are tender, which means they won't tolerate any frost. You can either start the seeds in a greenhouse or on a warm windowsill about 3 - 4 weeks before the last possible frost in your area, or wait until that date and sow the seeds out of doors under the protection of glass or plastic. (This could be a conventional cloche, a home-made cloche made from an old plastic drinks bottle, or some plastic 'fleece'.)

All the seeds should be sewn in individual pots, as the young plants are too delicate to tolerate being separated if grown in a large seed-tray. Cucumber seeds are small and can be sewn in 5cm (2") pots, but courgette, pumpkin and winter squash seeds need a 7 cm (3") pot. Any good seed compost will do, or you can do as I do and use Growbag compost. Another medium to start the seeds in is a grass turf, cut into squares and stood, grass side down, in a seed tray. The type of plastic net covered compost modules known as Jiffy pots are not suitable for these seeds, but other modular seed trays such as rigid 'plug-packs' or expanded polystyrene trays are suitable.

Put the seeds into the compost on their sides, and cover them with about their own width of compost. Keep the compost moist and protect the pots from mice, who are very fond of these seeds. You should see the seed-leaves emerge above the soil in 7 - 10 days.

When it comes to transplanting the young plants out of doors, cucumbers can be spaced at 30cm (12") intervals in rows 60cm (2 ft) apart, but all the others should be given much more space. Bush types (courgettes, Pattypans and some winter squash) need at least 1 metre (3' 3") between plants, and vine types need this same spacing between plants and between rows.

You can also grow cucumbers in Growbags, but most of the others require more growing medium and water supply than the average Growbag offers. I have grown cucumbers (3 plants) and Sweet Dumpling squash (1 plant) quite successfully in tubs 50cm (20") diameter, using compost from Growbags. I trained the vines up a teepee of bamboo canes to provide an attractive feature on my patio.

Cucumbers, courgettes and other summer squash should be planted where you can easily reach them to pick the fruit, which you will need to do every other day when they get into full production. Winter squash do not need to be picked until the fruits are ripe at the end of the season, so you don't need to worry about getting at individual plants.

The soil in your squash patch should be well composted and moist, as they are greedy feeders. Additional granular fertiliser can be given, both in the planting hole and raked into the surrounding soil. Vine types will root down wherever the trailers touch the soil, and they will soon cover the whole patch with greenery.

You don't have to hide your pumpkins or squash away - they can be used as ornamental plants. All courgettes have 'architectural' leaves, standing out away from the main stem, deeply cut and silvery tinged. Golden courgettes have a gold tinge to their leaves which makes for a very attractive 'spot' plant. Vine types offer scope for even more fun - they can be trained up supports, or even over tunnels or arches, where the fruits hang down like giant jewels. You may not think that the stems could be strong enough to allow a large pumpkin to dangle, but I have done this with all the vining types, and I promise you that the stem of even a 10 kilo (20 lb) squash is strong enough to keep it safe.

Problems

In very hot weather, the leaves will wilt by the end of the day. If they do not recover and look perky by the following morning, you should give them plenty of water. Many people fail to understand just how much water vegetables need when they are growing - it should be the equivalent of 3cm (1") rain per week, or 4 - 5 gallons per plant. Giant pumpkins grown for show need much more.

There are two main diseases likely to trouble you - powdery mildew and cucumber mosaic virus. Mildew can be controlled by spraying with a fungicide, but the virus is best dealt with by pulling out and destroying any affected plants before the disease spreads.

Picking

Cucumbers, courgettes and summer squashes should be cut with a sharp knife through the stem of the fruits, taking care not to sever the stem of the parent plant. Be careful to keep the cut ends away from your clothes, as they exude a clear liquid which sticks and cannot be removed. (I once ruined a good jumper by holding the hem out and using it to carry a load of courgettes.)

Winter squashes should be left on the plant as long as possible, so that they are really ripe before you pick them. The longer you can leave them, the better they will store. Normally, the leaves will start to wither and the plants will begin to look pretty sad by the end of the summer, and once the stems seem to have dried off you can cut the fruits. Cut them with a very sharp knife at the point where the stem of the fruit joins the plant, being careful not to lift the fruit away from the plant so that the 'handle' breaks off the fruit. If this does happen, use those fruits first, as they will not keep as long, tending to rot from the damaged end.

Once picked, the fruits should then be 'cured' by standing them in a greenhouse or other warm place. The ideal temperature is 25°C for about 10 days. This hardens the skin and seals the ends of the stems.

Storing

Store your crop of winter squashes in a cool dry place. The ideal temperature is 1°C and the ideal humidity is 75%. I keep mine in my (unheated) utility room, but a frost-free shed or cellar is equally good, as long as it is rodent proof.

Although the above is the ideal, you can keep them in a warmer place for several weeks, which will allow you to use them for decorations.

They don't have to be separated from each other - you can pile them up if you wish, but you should check them regularly in case any of them are starting to rot. The first sign of this is usually round the stem area, but sometimes depressed blemishes will appear on the skin. As soon as you see these signs, use those specimens straightaway. A fortnightly check for the first two months should be sufficient, but after that you should check them every week.

Fun for the children

While they are still growing, all the *Cucurbit* family react to wounds on their skins by exuding a liquid which forms a warty raised area. You can take advantage of this by writing children's names (or making patterns on specimens which you intend to use for decoration) with a blunt pencil while the fruits are still green. Then at harvest time, set the children loose in the pumpkin patch to find their own personal pumpkin!

Buying Pumpkins and Squash

Pumpkin

Pumpkins grow during the summer and are ready to harvest from early autumn - just in time for Hallowe'en in the Northern hemisphere. However, they are often available in big supermarkets from autumn through to late spring.

Miniature pumpkins are available under several named cultivars - Baby Boo, Jack Be Little or Munchkin - all of which are suitable for stuffing.

Medium sized pumpkins, such as Connecticut Field, Ghost Rider, Jack O'Lantern, or Small Sugar can be anything from 1 kilo (2 lbs) to 10 kilos (20 lbs) in weight. Most have golden skins, and will keep for four or five months. If you want a dual purpose pumpkin, which will give you easily hulled seeds as well as usable flesh, choose Godiva, or Triple Treat.

Large pumpkins, such as Hundredweight (with a pinkish skin) and Rouge Vif d'Etamps, (with a bright reddish-orange skin), weigh anything from 10 kilos (20 lbs) up. They will also keep well until you open them, after which you will have to use the flesh or cook and freeze it within a week.

Enormous pumpkins, such as Atlantic Giant, Show King or Sumo, are mainly intended for those who want to grow a real giant to win prizes. Despite what you may have heard, they are still edible, and some are quite flavoursome - but you're going to need a very large freezer if you want to go for the world record, which is, at the time of writing, approaching the 450 kilo (1000 lbs) mark!

I've never been able to detect much difference in flavour between any of the varieties of pumpkin, so choose your purchases by size. The smallest weigh about 125 g (4 - 5 oz) and are ideal for stuffing. Names include Baby Boo, Jack Be Little and Munchkin. Next come the size often called 'pie' pumpkins, weighing from 750 g (1½ lbs) to 2½ kilos (5 lbs), with names like Little Lantern or Small Sugar. Then the bigger varieties, from 3 to 25 kilos (6 to 50 lbs) such as Connecticut Field, Hundredweight, Jack O'Lantern, or the bright red Rouge Vif d'Etamps. Finally there are the giants, Atlantic Giant, Big Max or Sumo. These are generally supposed to be tasteless types suitable only for competition, but I grew Atlantic Giant one year and although my biggest was no more than 30 kilos (60 lbs) I found it tasted just as good as any of the smaller pumpkins.

Summer Squash

This category includes what are called courgettes in the UK and France and zucchini in America and Italy; pattypan squash; and the pale yellow Crookneck and Straightneck which are popular in America.

These grow during summer, and have a long harvesting period, from mid to late summer. However, they are available in supermarkets year round.

A courgette, by my definition, is a cylindrical fruit, which is either the same diameter all the way along, or may have a slight 'bell' at the end furthest from the stalk. Each seed company seems to have their own names for the different varieties - the only real difference is in the colour, which can be medium or dark green, very pale green (sometimes called 'white'), or golden. They all taste the same.

Pattypan squash, sometimes called Custard Marrow, also have many names, and also come in very pale green, gold, or dark green, and also all taste the same.

Summer squash are mainly yellow skinned, have a bell-shape, and may have a crooked 'neck' (the end nearest to the stalk). Some are knobbly skinned. They tend to be moister fleshed than courgettes.

Winter Squash

This is where the real variety of shapes, colours, sizes, and also textures and flavours appear. As a general rule, the types with softer flesh do not keep as well as those with denser hard flesh, so if you grow your own or buy a lot of squash at a farm shop or Pick Your Own outlet, these should be used first. They are harvested during autumn, but are available in supermarkets for a very long season. The two most popular varieties (with supermarket buyers, that is), Acorn and Butternut, are available almost year round, as they are grown in vast quantities in both hemispheres.

Perhaps I should explain that comment about supermarket buyers. There are two considerations here. The first is that apparently they have set a standard price-per-weight-unit for squash, regardless of variety. This would be fine if all varieties produced the same weight of fruit per hectare, but they don't. The two which are, to my mind, the most flavoursome, (Delicata and Sweet Dumpling) are in the 'low weight per hectare' category, so the big commercial growers are reluctant to grow them.

The second part of this is that the other really tasty varieties (Banana, Buttercup and Crown Prince) although 'high weight per hectare' are weighty fruits with tough skins. Since the average shopper only wants to buy a kilo or so at a time, this means the fruits have to be cut up before they can be displayed. That brings all sorts of logistical problems to the situation - the danger of supermarket staff cutting themselves when knives slip, the wrapping of the pieces, the fact that they only keep a couple of days after they've been cut - all of which would put the price up.

The answer to this, if you want to use these varieties of squash, is to bulk buy your season's supply at a farm shop or Pick Your Own farm, and store it at home.

I have indicated in most recipes which is the most appropriate type to use.

- **Acorn**. Looking more like a segmented ox-heart than an acorn, these are single coloured (dark green, white or gold), and weigh about 1 kilo (2 lbs). They are hard skinned and keep well. They are useful for baking whole or stuffing. Most are cream fleshed, although some can be yellow. They have a delicate chestnut flavour which goes well with fish as well as mild cheeses and chicken. Cultivar names include Table Ace and Table Queen. They are freely available in shops.

- **Banana**. A large pink cylindrical squash weighing up to 25 kilos (50 lbs). Flesh is orange, but with a high water content, so more suitable for soups than baking. More likely to be found on market stalls than in supermarkets.

- **Buttercup**. Almost square, these are dark green with some slight paler striping and a large depression at the flower end. They weigh in at about 3 - 4 kilos (6 - 8 lbs). They have very dense sweet golden flesh, excellent for serving as plain mash, or for baking. More likely to be found in farm shops or Pick Your Own farms than supermarkets.

- **Butternut**. A smooth-skinned pale beige squash, with one end belled and the other cylindrical. The bell end contains the seeds, while the other end is solid flesh, making them useful for dishes which require evenly-shaped slices. Sweet fleshed, they are suitable for puddings as well as savoury dishes. They are freely available in shops and supermarkets. Some small versions are now available, but these are less well flavoured than the larger ones, which usually weigh about 1 kilo (2 lbs)

- **Calabaza**. A large round or pear-shaped squash from the West Indies, these have a mottled green and orange skin and orange flesh. You're more likely to find this one on market stalls than in supermarkets. It's good for grating, or using in meat or fish stews as well as any of the dishes that need purée.

- **Crown Prince**. Considered by some to be the best variety, it has dense gold flesh, and is an extremely good keeper. I've kept them for up to 8 months. A flat round fruit with fairly hard, pale green/grey skin and gold flesh, they weigh in at around 3 - 4 kilos (6 - 8 lbs). They are beginning to be more freely available.

- **Delicata**, sometimes called 'potato' squash. They weigh about 750 g (1½ lbs), and are cylindrical, with skin that is almost white with green stripes and speckles when first picked, but turns yellow with gold markings as they mature in storage. They are extremely good keepers - up to 8 months. A new version called Sugar Loaf is now available, slightly smaller with rounder fruits. The flesh is sweet and chestnutty flavoured. Beginning to be more freely available in supermarkets, but you may have to go to a Pick Your Own farm for them.

- **Gem**, sometimes called Rolet. Dark green or gold tennis ball sized squash with flesh rather like Acorn. Very tough skinned, they are quite good keepers and freely available in supermarkets. Their small size makes them useful for stuffing.

- **Gold Nugget**. An early-maturing, soft-fleshed squash, with a flattish round shape and gold skin. Very tough skinned, they are best baked whole before the seeds are removed. They are not very good keepers, lasting only 6 - 8 weeks. They weigh about 1 kilo (2 lbs) and are freely available in supermarkets.

- **Hubbard**. Hard skinned, usually bright orange, but also available in dark green. The flesh is deep gold and particularly useful for baked dishes such as cakes and breads.

Keeps up to 6 months. This is the one most likely to be offered by non-specialist seed companies, but because it is quite large at 3 - 4 kilos (6 - 8 lbs), you are less likely to find it in the supermarkets.

- **Kabocha**. A small squash with hard green or red skin, this has fairly soft flesh. Most specimens available in shops will be about 1 kilo (2 lbs). Quite a good keeper, it can be used for most of the dishes that follow.

- **Muscade de Provence**. An attractive squash with large flat-topped round, deeply scalloped fruits. It is a very good keeper, green when harvested, turning brown with maturity. The flesh is quite sweet, so use it for puddings, jams and sweets as well as soups.

- **Sweet Dumpling**. Short and squat, weighing about 500 g (1 lb), this is sometimes offered in seed catalogues as 'edible gourd'. Rather like a sweet pepper in shape, they are almost white with green stripes and speckles when first picked, but turn yellow with gold markings as they mature in storage. They are extremely good keepers - up to 8 months. The flesh is sweet and chestnutty, very like Delicata. You're unlikely to find them in supermarkets, but they are extensively grown on Pick Your Own farms.

- **Triamble**. Usually mid to pale green, this squash has a curious three-lobed shape. The flesh is orange and dense, so useful for most dishes. It will keep for up to 6 months, but you're unlikely to find it for sale unless you go to a specialist grower or grow it yourself.

- **Turk's Cap**. This is a flat round squash, orange skinned with green and white stripes, and a protruding top which makes it look like a turban. It keeps well, and has orange flesh which is good for baked dishes, or soups. It's attractive shape makes it particularly good for use as a soup tureen. It is sometimes available in supermarkets, but more likely to be found at farm shops.

- **Uchiki Kuri**, sometimes known as Onion squash. These are small bright orange squash, with a good flavoured but quite watery flesh. Excellent for soup or stuffing, they should be used quickly as they don't keep for more than a few weeks.

Cucumbers

Unless you grow your own, cucumbers are long dark green cylinders. They should feel stiff rather than flabby. Opinions vary on whether peeling them makes any difference to their 'burp' factor - I don't think it does, but then they don't affect me like that anyway. Gardeners who fancy something different can grow the variety 'Crystal Apple' which is egg-sized, whitish in colour and spherical.

Marrows

You may wonder why there are no recipes in this book for vegetable marrows. The answer is simple - I regard them as no more than seriously over-grown courgettes, tasteless and watery, and fit only for the compost heap. Yes, I know you can stuff them with something interesting, but you can also put that stuffing into something that has a decent taste and texture, so why waste it on a marrow?

If you must, they are available from autumn to late winter in supermarkets.

Vegetable spaghetti (spaghetti squash)

Until very recently there was only one variety of this, with very pale greeny-white plain or green striped and speckled skin and white flesh. Now there is a new type called Orangetti, with orange skin and orange flesh which has a high vitamin A content.

They are harvested in late autumn, but are available in supermarkets until early spring.

Choosing which specimen to buy

Whole fruits. Some varieties have naturally warty skins, so don't worry about this. The fruit should feel firm and heavy for its size. Reject flabby feeling fruits. See the details on individual varieties for those which keep well, and buy these in autumn when they will be considerably cheaper than later. Some varieties will keep for up to six months in a cool dry place.

Wedges. As well as feeling heavy, with a firm skin, the flesh itself should be dense and firm. Avoid pieces which have stringy-looking flesh. It is better to buy a piece with the seeds still in, as removing them shortens the storage time.

Do take the trouble to buy the varieties recommended for each type of recipe, especially winter squash. There is a considerable variation in the moisture content of flesh, and using, for instance, a wet-fleshed variety where the recipe calls for a dry-fleshed variety may not give the right result.

Don't try to lift pumpkins or winter squash by the stalk, as it could break off, and leave an open patch which is then vulnerable to rot.

Pumpkins and Squash for Decoration

Everyone knows you can carve pumpkins into Hallowe'en lanterns, but not everyone thinks of using them in other ways for decoration. Pumpkins, and more particularly winter squashes, come in such a variety of shapes, sizes and colours, that if you do no more than pile them up in a large dish you will have an attractive display.

But you can do more:

- wire small specimens into wreaths and other autumn flower displays.
- hollow larger specimens out to use as flower containers or candle holders.
- hollow them out to use a food holders - either large specimens to hold soup or risotto, smaller specimens for dips or sauces.
- use metal threads, chains and studs to decorate individual specimens with stripes or patterns, in the same way as you would decorate an orange with cloves to make a pomander.
- add paint and other enhancements to make 'animals' - for instance, crook-neck summer squash make convincing 'geese' with a coat of white paint overall, yellow on the stem for the beak and button eyes.
- dry suitable specimens in a very slow oven and enhance them with carving.

Hallowe'en lanterns

Once you have removed the seeds and disturbed the flesh of your pumpkin, it will deteriorate very quickly, so do not make the lantern more than a day ahead of when you intend to use it. (As long as you leave sufficient flesh to keep the skin rigid, there is no reason why you should not use the flesh you've removed for cooking.)

Small children should be supervised during the carving operation, as the tough skin of the pumpkin may make the knife slip. Cut a large lid so that you can get your whole hand inside for ease of movement, then pull out the seeds and their strings. Then scoop out the flesh to make as large a cavity as you need. The best implement for this operation is a melon baller.

Then use a felt-tipped pen to mark the 'face' or other design on the skin and remove first the outer skin, then the flesh behind it, a little at a time. Once the skin has gone, the melon baller can be used again to remove the skin behind. When the lantern is finished, place it in its display position and put in a small squat candle or night-light. Light it through the carved aperture with a long match or spill.

Preparation for Cooking

Courgettes, summer squash, Pattypans and immature specimens of pumpkin and other winter squash varieties

Most of these do not need to be peeled, and indeed should not be peeled, as there is a layer of stronger flavour immediately under the skin. The colour of the skin also adds to the look of the dish, especially when you use a mixture of different coloured specimens (for instance, dark green and gold courgettes). Whether you need to peel immature specimens of winter squashes will depend on how immature they are, and that's something you'll learn by experience - but as a rough guide, if you press a fingernail on the skin, and it takes pressure to go through, you should peel.

Long specimens which you are going to cut into rondels can be visually enhanced by scoring lengthways with a fork or cannel knife to remove narrow strips of skin before cutting.

If you intend to stuff any of these, obviously you will have to remove the central seed-carrying part. Whether or not you need to do so otherwise, once again depends on the degree of immaturity. My view is that a courgette with a diameter of more than 3cm (1") or length of more than 15cm (6") has gone too far - but then I grow my own which does tend to make me pickier than I might be if I had to buy them. The real test is to chop off a slice and see how advanced the seed development is. If they look as though the seeds have shells and the fibres round them are getting stringy, you should get rid of them.

Some *Cucurbita* family members, especially immature specimens, exude a clear liquid when they are cut. Take care to keep this liquid off your clothes, as it sets hard and will not wash out. Squash that do this should not be de-gorged with salt, as they may absorb a lot of the salt in the process and will end up too salty for savoury dishes and useless for sweet ones.

Depending on the recipe, you may want to de-gorge some of these summer varieties.

Mature pumpkins and winter squash (except spaghetti squash)

Unless you intend to stuff these, you will need to remove the skin. In some cases, where the recipe calls for purée, you can do this after the preliminary cooking stage. (This applies if you bake, microwave or steam large pieces or whole fruits - in which case all you do is cook the piece and let it cool down before scraping out the flesh.)

Some varieties can be peeled with an ordinary vegetable peeler, but others have tough skins and you will find it easier to use a knife to remove the skin. In all cases it is sensible to reduce whole fruits or large wedges to smaller pieces for ease of handling - but even, that can be difficult with the varieties which have very tough skins.

Be aware that very tough skins may cause the knife to slip, and always make the first cut so that a slipping knife will not come your way. The easiest way to get into a tough-skinned variety is to spread a couple of newspapers on the kitchen floor and drop the fruit on them from waist height. This will open it enough to get a knife in, even if it doesn't actually break it into several pieces.

With any variety which has a segmented shape, such as Acorn or the French Muscade de Provence, make your cuts down the depressions to cut it into its natural segments.

Having reduced the fruit into manageable pieces, remove the obvious outer skin and any inner layer which is a different colour from the inner flesh.

All pumpkins and winter squash should have the seeds, and the stringy fibre which surrounds them, removed. If you want to keep the seeds, postpone extracting them from the fibre until you have finished the other preparation, as this will make your hands wet and sticky.

Don't be tempted to save the seeds from squash for growing your own. They will grow, easily enough, but unless you have grown the squash yourself, in total isolation from any other member of the *Cucurbita* family (pumpkin, squash, marrow, melon, cucumber, ornamental gourd) you are unlikely to get the same thing. This whole family of plants is notoriously promiscuous, and they cross-breed and hybridise easily. The end result will normally be pretty tasteless.

If you are into making your own vegetable stock, the skin, seeds and stringy filaments of the seed-covering make a good rich stock.

Peeling and de-seeding a whole or part raw pumpkin reduces the weight by about one-third - thus a 250g (8 oz) piece will give about 175g (6 oz) of usable flesh when peeled and de-seeded.

Spaghetti squash

These squash should be cooked whole before removing the seeds or skin. Prick the squash a few times with a skewer, then either bake it in a moderate oven for an hour, or steam or boil it for 30 - 40 minutes. Let it cool completely before cutting it in half longitudinally, scraping out first the seeds, then the spaghetti-like strands of flesh. The easiest way to do this is to tease the strands apart with a fork while they are still in the skin. Once cooked, these strands can be kept for up to 48 hours in a refrigerator.

Preparing squash or pumpkins for stuffing

Wipe the squash clean and start by deciding which way up it should go. In general, they should sit on the stalk end, as this is flattest, but if you want to put the top back, it may be better to use them the other way up so that the stalk forms a 'handle' for the lid. You may need to remove a sliver of flesh from the bottom to provide a flat base for it to stand on.

Start by inserting a knife angled inwards so that the piece you remove will sit back on afterwards, then cut round and remove the 'lid'. Reach in, pull out the seeds and their fibres, then with a sharp implement, scoop out the rest of the fibres, then more flesh if you need a bigger hole.

The sharp implement could be a spoon, a melon baller, or a butter curler (remember them? You drag them over the top of the butter and they produce a dainty little curl of butter. I haven't seen them in the shops lately, but they are ideal for this job.)

Using a pumpkin or big squash as a container for soup

This is a really impressive way to serve pumpkin soup at a dinner party, using a hollowed-out pumpkin as a soup tureen. Choose a pumpkin with a flat base and with its stalk still attached, cutting the lid out from this end. If you prefer the flavour of squash, use a Turk's Cap squash, cutting the nubbly top as a lid rather than the stem end, but remove the stalk so that the squash will sit flat in the dish.

Cut a 'lid' from the top of the pumpkin, angling the knife inwards to provide a good seat for the lid. Scoop out and discard the seeds and stringy filaments in the middle of the pumpkin, then, using a melon baller, carefully scoop out the flesh, leaving at least half an inch inside the skin. The bigger the squash, the thicker the wall should be.

Set the hollow pumpkin aside and prepare the soup to the simmering stage.

Pre-heat the oven to 450°F (230°C) Gas Mark 8.

Place the pumpkin shell in an fairly deep oven-proof serving dish. When the soup is hot, pour it into the pumpkin, replace the 'lid', cover the tin with cooking foil and bake it in the oven for 30 - 40 minutes.

To serve, remove the foil, loosen the pumpkin lid with a knife, lift it and grate nutmeg on the surface. Replace the lid before taking it to the table. When you've served all the soup from the pumpkin, you can scrape the remaining flesh out of the skin if you wish.

Variation - instead of cooking the container as well as the contents, you can use a raw squash shell as a serving dish. The only problem with this is that it will cool down the contents unless you warm it first, so before filling it with soup or risotto, fill it with boiling water and let it stand for a few minutes, then empty out the water and put in the soup.

If you are artistically inclined, choose a green-skinned squash and carve patterns in the skin, deep enough to show the orange flesh beneath. Don't try to do this if you intend cooking the shell, as the carved areas won't be strong enough to hold the contents.

Storing pumpkin flesh

Once you have cut a pumpkin or squash open, you have a few days to do something with the unused portion before it starts to rot. I usually wrap it in cling-film and store it in the fridge (if it is a small piece) or in my cool utility room (if it is an enormous specimen). If you do this, you should leave the seeds in as removing them invites the rotting to start straight away. I have kept raw squash and pumpkin for up to a week like this, and on one occasion when I forgot about the chunk of a particularly big brute lurking on top of a high shelf, for two weeks. It had started to go wrong on the cut edges, but when I cut off a thick slice I found it was all right underneath.

Cooked squash or pumpkin can be kept safely in the fridge for 24 hours, but if you intend to keep it for longer, it is better to freeze it as purée. It keeps well in the freezer for up to three months, but starts to deteriorate in texture and taste after that.

Preparing pumpkin or squash purée

These are the basic methods of making pumpkin or squash purée, regardless of the variety. However, with the waterier varieties, such as plain pumpkin, and also depending on what you intend to do with the purée, you may want to degorge the flesh to get rid of some of the liquid before you cook it. It is also advisable to drain the cooked flesh, and sometimes also the actual purée, in a fine-meshed sieve. Don't throw the cooking water away - it makes wonderful vegetable stock.

Boiling

Unless you intend to make soup, never boil pumpkin or squash or you will end up with a watery mush.

Method One

Peel and deseed and slice the fruit. Cut it into chunks and either:

- put it in a dish or plastic bag in the microwave and cook it on High for 5 - 10 minutes, then test it with a skewer to see if it is done. If not, cook again on High in increments of 2 minutes until it is done.
- put in a steamer and steam it for 10 minutes, then test with a skewer as above.

Method Two

If you are dealing with a small specimen, leave it whole but prick it with a skewer a few times. If you are dealing with a large specimen, cut it into wedges and remove the seeds and their fibres. Then either:

- put it in a dish or plastic bag in the microwave and treat it as above.
- put it in an oven-proof dish and bake it for 45 - 50 minutes at 400°F (200°C) Gas Mark 6.

Allow it to cool until it is handleable and scrape out the flesh.

Once the flesh is cooked, just put it in a bowl or empty saucepan and mash it to the desired consistency. Small quantities can be puréed in a food processor.

A Note on Ingredients

- **Butter** - yes, I know it's meant to be the wrong sort of fat and bad for you, but my view is that I would rather trust cows than chemists, and I personally prefer the taste. If you don't agree with me, substitute margarine where I've said butter.

- **Cream** - as above, I like the real thing. If you really are concerned about fat levels, you can substitute yoghurt, either completely or in whatever proportion seems right to you. Where the cream has to be whipped, mixtures work best if you whip the cream first to just short of the stage you need it at for the dish, then gradually add the yoghurt while whipping until you achieve the final desired texture.

- **Eggs** - unless otherwise stated, eggs are size 3 (medium).

- **Olive oil** - I have to be careful what I say here, as my editor wrote the definitive book on olive oil, but whilst it is always a good idea to use good quality oil, ie Extra Virgin, there is little point in using a delicately flavoured estate-bottled oil for frying, since all the delicate flavour will disappear in the process. Save these expensive oils for salad dressings, or for adding to soups or stews just before serving.

- **Milk** - as above, I prefer the taste of real milk, and the only sort I buy is what my local supermarket calls 'breakfast' milk, ie full-fat milk from Channel Islands cows. If you want to use one of the lower fat varieties, that's up to you.

- **Pepper** - unless otherwise stated, 'pepper' always means 'freshly ground black pepper'.

- **Pumpkin seed oil** - I haven't specified this in any of the recipes, as the only use I have found for it so far is in salad dressing. It has to be refined to reduce its reddish brown colour to a more acceptable yellow, and in this process loses its smell. It tastes quite sweet.

- **Quinoa** - this is a non-cereal grain which you cook in the same way as rice. However, it is gluten-free, which means it is suitable for people with gluten allergies, and it is also very high in protein, (20% or double the amount in wheat). One other advantage it has over rice is that it does not stick. A tiny golden grain, it swells to 3 times the bulk when cooked, and the germ separates, giving a pretty spiral effect.

- **Stock** - In all the recipes that don't involve meat in any other form, vegetarians can use vegetable stock instead of meat-based stock.

Servings

All recipes, unless otherwise stated, are for four people - which means four average eaters, or two greedy ones!

Metric/Imperial measures

One of the complications of writing recipes these days is that you have to give weights and other measurements in both metric and imperial form, which inevitably leads to some anomalies unless you use cumbersomely precise conversions (eg 1 oz = 28.375 g). These are then very difficult to measure.

I've opted for a non-cumbersome set of conversions, so you'll have to forgive me for saying that while 25 g is 1 oz, 250 g is 8 oz.

But then experienced cooks know that cooking is not a matter of precise measurements, but of tastes and textures and minor adjustments to achieve results in the way you personally like them.

Winter Squash

Soups and stews

Pumpkin and squash soups

Presentation and garnishes

Pumpkins and winter squashes make thick creamy textured soups. Their colour ranges from pale browny-gold to deep red (with added tomato), and they all look good when garnished with a contrasting colour. For the deep coloured soups, this could be a dollop of thick yoghurt or crème fraîche or a spoonful of thin cream or buttermilk swirled on top; for the paler coloured soups it could be a red tomato-based sauce or a green herb or chilli-based sauce. Choose from the sauces or other garnishes shown below.

All squash soups benefit from a grating of fresh nutmeg on top just before serving.

Apple confit

1 tablespoon unsalted butter
2 apples, peeled, cored and sliced
100 ml (4 fl oz) apple juice
1 tablespoon Calvados (optional)

Sauté the butter and apple for 5 minutes, add the apple juice and cook for 15 minutes to soften the apple and reduce the liquid. Mash or purée to a coarse texture, then stir in the Calvados, if using. Swirl a generous spoonful round the top of each bowlful of soup before serving.

Sun-dried tomato sauce

4 halves sun-dried tomatoes
4 tablespoons boiling water
3 tablespoons olive oil

Soak the tomatoes in the boiling water for 10 minutes, then whizz them in the blender with the olive oil. Sieve before serving. Add a generous spoonful swirled round the top of each bowlful of soup.

Green chilli and coriander chutney

2 green chillies, coarsely chopped
4 tablespoons water
a pinch of salt
50 g (2 oz) chopped blanched almonds
leaves from ¹/₂ bunch fresh coriander (or parsley)

Whizz everything in the blender to a fine texture. Store in the refrigerator until needed. You can make this sauce up to a day in advance of using it. Serve a bowlful so that diners can help themselves to a spoonful.

Garnishes for pumpkin and squash soups

Sprinkle any of these on top of the soup:
- chopped toasted hazelnuts
- pumpkin seeds
- spring onion, chopped
- maple syrup
- croûtons

Cream of pumpkin, potato and leek soup

Delicately flavoured by leeks, given body by potato, and sharpened up by the black pepper and nutmeg sprinkled on top when you serve it, this soup is substantial enough to make a meal on its own with some good brown bread.

250 g (8 oz) prepared pumpkin
100 g (4 oz) potato
100 g (4 oz) leeks (white portions only)
1 clove garlic, chopped
2-3 tablespoons olive oil
1 litre (2 pints) chicken or vegetable stock
300 ml (10 fl oz) single cream
salt
pepper
nutmeg, grated

Chop the pumpkin into chunks. Peel the potato and chop into chunks the same size as the pumpkin flesh, clean the leeks and chop the white bits into rondels.

Fry the garlic in the oil in a large saucepan for a couple of minutes. Add the pumpkin, potato and leek to the saucepan with the garlic and oil, put the lid on and let the vegetables sweat for about 20 minutes, checking half-way through to ensure they don't go dry and stick. If this seems imminent, add some of the stock.

Add half of the stock and bring it to the boil, then simmer until the vegetables are soft. Let them cool a little and reduce them to a purée in a liquidizer or food processor. Return them to the saucepan, add the rest of the stock, season to taste and return to simmering point for another 10 minutes before stirring in the cream and serving with nutmeg and pepper sprinkled on top.

Pumpkin and white bean soup

Pumpkin and beans is one of the happy marriages of flavours, giving the sort of earthy taste that many people, including me, think of as comfort food. This soup can't be made in a hurry, because the beans have to be soaked overnight, then cooked separately before adding the other vegetables, but the end product is well worth the wait.

---

175 g (6 oz) dried haricot or butter beans
2 litres (4 pints) water
5 fresh sage leaves
1 bay leaf
2 cloves garlic
2 stems fresh thyme
3 tablespoons olive oil
3 leeks, finely chopped
2 carrots, finely chopped
2 stalks celery, finely chopped
500 g (1 lb) prepared pumpkin, in small chunks
salt
parsley to garnish

Put the beans in a saucepan, boil half the water and pour it over the beans. Leave them to soak overnight. Next day, drain the beans and put them in fresh water, bring them up to the boil, add 3 of the sage leaves, 1 of the garlic cloves (whole), the bay leaf and the thyme. Do not add salt, or the beans will not soften. Simmer until the beans are soft - about 30 minutes. Drain them, retaining the water.

Prepare the other vegetables, starting by cleaning them well to ensure no dirt remains. Put all the peelings and the pumpkin seeds in a big saucepan with the water from the beans and the rest of the water. Bring this to the boil and simmer it for about 30 minutes. Strain it, discarding the solid residue, and you have the stock for your soup.

Chop or crush the second garlic clove and fry it, with the oil in your soup pan with the leek, carrot, celery and pumpkin, for 5 minutes. Add the beans and about a third of the stock, bring it to the boil and simmer until the vegetables are tender.

Liquidize the mixture to your preferred texture, put it back in the saucepan, season it to your taste and add more stock. You may not need it all unless you like a thin soup. Bring the soup back to boiling point before serving it, garnished with chopped parsley.

Winter squash soup

If you are really fond of the flavour of winter squash, you can make soup by doing no more than adding liquid to mashed squash (now you know what to do with the left-overs). But add an onion and some spices, and you have a much more flavoursome soup, as suitable for a smart dinner party as for your private supper on a cold night.

12 coriander seeds
12 black peppercorns
10cm (3") cinnamon stick
8 cloves
2 small dried chillies
1 tablespoon chopped mint
450 ml (3/4 pint) milk
50 g (2 oz) butter
1 medium onion, chopped finely
1 kilo (2 lbs) flesh of a dense squash such as Buttercup,
    Crown Prince or Hubbard
600 ml (1 pint) water
salt

Infuse the spices and mint in the milk by putting them all in a saucepan and heating it until the milk is just short of boiling, then take it off the heat and leave it to stand for 30 minutes. Strain and discard the spices and mint.

In your soup pan, melt the butter and fry the onion until it is translucent. Chop the squash and add it to the pan with the water, bring it to the boil and simmer until the squash is tender - about 15 minutes.

Liquidize the mixture and return it to the pan with the spiced milk. Bring it back to simmering point and add salt to your taste. Simmer for 5 minutes before serving.

Simple Butternut squash soup

Here's the answer to what you do with the bell-end of a Butternut squash that you have left over from another dish where you have used the seedless piece - you make it into soup. Pleasant but fairly bland in taste, this is one of the soups that benefits from a contrasting tasted garnish, such as sun-dried tomato sauce, or chopped green chillies.

1 medium onion, chopped
1 tablespoon olive oil
500 g (1 lb) prepared Butternut squash
600 ml (1 pint) chicken or vegetable stock
salt

In your soup pan, slowly cook the onion in the oil until it has turned translucent.

Chop the squash flesh into small chunks and add them to the soup pan with enough stock to cover, bring it to the boil and simmer until the squash is tender - about 15 minutes.

Purée the soup, add more stock to bring it to your desired texture, season it to taste, and reheat before serving.

Optional variations

- add 2 - 3 cloves of garlic, finely chopped.
- replace some or all of the stock with buttermilk.
- if you want a sweet soup, add 50 g (2 oz) cranberries and 50 g (2 oz) granulated sugar.
- add the juice and zest of 1 lime or ½ lemon, and garnish with chopped fresh sage.

Butternut squash and apple soup

This is one of the classic squash soups. The apple off-sets the blandness of the squash to a certain degree, but in my opinion it still needs something contrasting as a garnish. Apple confit with Calvados is my first choice, but sun-dried tomato sauce is almost as good.

---

1 medium onion, chopped
1 tablespoon olive oil
500 g (1 lb) prepared Butternut squash
2 cooking apples, ideally Bramleys, peeled and cored
600 ml (1 pint) chicken or vegetable stock
salt
white pepper
apple confit to garnish

In your soup pan, slowly cook the onion in the oil until it has turned translucent.

Chop the squash flesh and apples into small chunks and add them to the soup pan with enough stock to cover, bring it to the boil and simmer until the squash is tender - about 15 minutes.

Purée the soup, add more stock to bring it to your desired texture, season it to taste, and reheat before serving.

Optional variations

- if you want a sweet soup, add 50 g (2 oz) cranberries and 50 g (2 oz) granulated sugar.

Butternut squash and orange soup

With wine and orange juice, this is a rich soup which is more suited to small servings at the beginning of a dinner party than large servings for a casual family supper. Rich or not, it introduces yet another range of flavours to the creaminess of Butternut squash.

500 g (1 lb) prepared Butternut squash
1 medium onion, chopped
1 tablespoon olive oil
1/2 teaspoon powdered ginger
4 tablespoons dry white wine
250 ml (8 fl oz) orange juice
600 ml (1 pint) chicken or vegetable stock
salt
white pepper
120 ml (4 fl oz) double cream

Chop the squash into small chunks and fry them with the onion in the oil until both are soft. Stir in the ginger, cook for 2 minutes, then stir in the wine and cook until the liquid has reduced by half.

Whizz the mixture in the liquidizer to a smooth purée and return it to the saucepan.

Add the orange juice and stock, bring the soup back to the boil, taste and season it then simmer for 5 minutes. Serve it with a swirl of double cream in each bowl.

Pumpkin and bacon soup

Pumpkin soup, without the addition of some fairly strong flavour, can be rather bland. On the other hand, you can go too far and add something which is so assertive that you might just as well not have bothered to include pumpkin at all. In this pumpkin soup, the flavour comes from celery, bacon and a little curry powder, which enhances the delicate pumpkin taste without totally submerging it.

1 kilo (2 lbs) prepared pumpkin
1 stalk celery, chopped fairly small
2 large carrots, chopped fairly small
900 ml (1 1/2 pints) chicken stock
1 medium onion, chopped
250 g (8 oz) bacon, diced
1 tablespoon sunflower oil
1 teaspoon curry powder
1 tablespoon plain flour
salt
nutmeg

Cut the pumpkin into small chunks and cook it with the celery and carrot in about half of the stock until tender. Liquidize.

Meanwhile, fry the onion and bacon in the oil until both are translucent. Add the curry powder and flour and stir them in so that all the onion and bacon is coated, then add the remaining stock a little at a time, stirring, so that the mixture thickens without developing lumps.

Add the liquidized vegetables, bring all to the boil and simmer for 5 minutes. Taste and season if necessary. (This will be dependant on the saltiness of the bacon.) Simmer another 5 minutes before serving with a grating of nutmeg on top.

Acorn squash and coconut soup

Adding coconut cream to the creamy texture of Acorn squash gives this soup an unctuous feel. Serve it for a special dinner party, or even for a seduction supper - or just when you feel entitled to a little pampering.

You can use tinned coconut cream, but I find this can be a bit grainy, so I prefer to use the solid blocks of creamed coconut.

---

1 tablespoon olive oil
2 small onions or 4 shallots, chopped finely
1 teaspoon powdered ginger
flesh of 3 Acorn squash, puréed
900 ml (1 1/2 pints) chicken or vegetable stock
100 g (4 oz) solid creamed coconut
salt
white pepper
50 g (2 oz) toasted coconut flesh (ideally curls)

Heat the oil and fry the onions until they are translucent. Stir in the powdered ginger, then draw the pan off the heat and stir in the squash purée. Gradually add the stock.

Bring the soup back to simmering heat, then grate in the coconut cream and stir until it is dissolved. Season to your taste and simmer a further 5 minutes before serving garnished with the toasted coconut.

Pumpkin and prawn soup

Here is a soup which you can whizz up very quickly if you have prawns in your freezer. My cat insists that there should always be prawns available in case he feels like a snack, so this is a soup we have quite often. (We also eat a lot of prawn cocktails, but that's another story.)

---

3 small onions, chopped
1 tablespoon olive oil
1 teaspoon powdered ginger .
300 ml (1/2 pint) chicken stock
500 g (1 lb) pumpkin purée
400 - 500 g (1 lb) frozen prawns, thawed
salt
white pepper

Fry the onions in the oil until they are translucent, then stir in the powdered ginger. Gradually add some of the stock, then the pumpkin purée and most of the prawns, keeping a few for garnishing. Transfer to a liquidizer and whizz until the mixture is fairly smooth. Return it to the saucepan and add the rest of the stock.

Bring it to the boil and simmer for 5 minutes, season it to your taste and simmer for 2 - 3 minutes more before serving. Pop a few prawns on top of each serving.

Squash and tomato soup

Strictly speaking, this ought to be called tomato and squash soup, since it is the tomato flavour which predominates. Never mind, the end result is excellent, and adding the squash does solve the problem of over-acidity which tends to haunt home-made tomato soups. It is still a little on the sharp side though, so it needs a generous swirl of cream when you serve it.

---

1 tablespoon olive oil
1 medium onion, chopped
2 cloves garlic, finely chopped
1 kilo (2 lbs) squash, ideally Crown Prince, Hubbard
    or Kabocha
900 ml (1½ pints) chicken or vegetable stock
500 g (1 lb) homemade tomato sauce, or purchased passata
salt
pepper
250 ml (8 fl oz) single cream

Fry the onion and garlic in the oil until they are translucent. Chop the squash into small chunks. Add the squash and about half of the stock to the pan and cook until tender. Liquidize and return to the pan with the rest of the stock and the passata.

Bring the mixture back to the boil and simmer for 5 minutes, then taste and season. Simmer another 5 minutes before serving with a generous swirl of cream in each bowl.

Pumpkin and lentil stew (p36)

Succotash

Succotash is an original Native American dish. It is a happy marriage of the three 'sister' plants which are traditionally grown together - corn, beans and pumpkins, each plant supplying its neighbours with their needs in a clever horticultural symbiosis. The corn provided a support for the climbing beans, the beans provided nitrogen for the corn and the pumpkins, and the pumpkins provided shade at the roots to keep the ground moist, then later the prickles on the pumpkin leaf stalks deterred the animals that would otherwise steal the corn and the beans.

It doesn't really matter what sort of beans you use, but a white-skinned type such as butterbeans or haricot beans will give a better colour - or rather will not stain the succotash with their skin colour.

250 g (8 oz) prepared pumpkin flesh
50 g (2 oz) butter
1 small onion, finely chopped
half a red pepper, finely chopped
100 g (4 oz) dried beans, soaked and pre-cooked
250 g (8 oz) sweetcorn
250 ml (8 fl oz) water
salt
pepper

Cut the pumpkin flesh into walnut-sized chunks. In a saucepan, melt the butter and fry the onion and pepper until the onion is translucent. Add the pumpkin, beans, sweetcorn and water, bring to the boil, turn the heat down and simmer, covered, for 10 minutes. Season and simmer a further 5 minutes.

Serve with freshly baked wholemeal bread.

Optional variations

- stir 3 tablespoons single cream in at the end of cooking.
- crumble two rashers of crisply cooked streaky bacon over each serving.
- include 1 green chilli pepper at the frying stage.
- sprinkle chopped parsley on top before serving.
- substitute 2 tablespoons sweet paprika for the black pepper.

Spaghetti squash primavera (p47)

Thai-style pumpkin and prawn soup-stew

I call this recipe a soup-stew because you can either serve it as a runny stew, or fish out the solids with a perforated spoon to serve with rice and serve the liquid as soup alongside. Whichever way you do it, the result is excellent.

If you can't get fresh lemon grass, use dried but soak it in boiling water first. Alternatively, use 1 teaspoon lemon zest.

---

1 tablespoon vegetable oil
1 clove garlic, crushed
4 spring onions, chopped
2 small red chillies, de-seeded and chopped
1 stem fresh lemon grass, halved and cut into 4 pieces
1/2 teaspoon shrimp paste
250 ml (8 fl oz) hot chicken stock
500 g (1 lb) prepared pumpkin, in 3cm (1") cubes
1/2 block solid coconut cream, grated
250 g (8 oz) small prawns
salt
pepper
chopped basil to garnish

Heat the oil and fry the garlic and onion until they are soft, then add the lemon grass, chillies and shrimp paste and fry, stirring, for 2 minutes. Add the chicken stock and bring the mixture to the boil before adding the pumpkin. Wait until the liquid has returned to the boil, then turn down the heat and simmer for 10 minutes.

Add the coconut milk and prawns and cook for a further 5 minutes.

Season, and cook another 5 minutes before serving, garnished with the chopped basil leaves.

Butternut squash and quinoa stew

This dish makes a good filling meal, with plenty of taste. It's pretty to look at too, as the grains of quinoa look like pearls, contrasting with the chunks of vegetable. All it needs as an accompaniment is some good brown bread, or for a crunchy texture contrast you could serve it with baked potato skins.

250 g (8 oz) potatoes
1 large Bramley apple, peeled and cored
500 g (1 lb) prepared Butternut squash
2 tablespoons olive oil
1 onion, sliced
2 cloves garlic, finely chopped
2 teaspoons cumin seeds
2 tablespoons paprika
400 g tin chopped tomatoes
250 ml (8 fl oz) red wine (e.g. French vin de pays)
600 ml (1 pint) vegetable stock
100 g (4 oz) quinoa
salt
pepper
yoghurt or crème fraîche

Chop the potatoes, apple and squash into walnut-sized chunks.

In a large saucepan, heat the oil and fry the onion and garlic until they are translucent. Add the cumin seeds and paprika and cook another 2 minutes, then stir in the potatoes, apple and squash. Cook them for a couple of minutes, turning them over so that they are coated with the spices, then pour in the tomatoes, wine and stock.

Bring it to the boil, then turn down the heat and simmer for 15 minutes. Season, then stir in the quinoa. Continue to simmer, stirring occasionally, until the liquid has almost gone and the quinoa is tender. Serve it in deep soup plates or bowls, with a dollop of yoghurt or crème fraîche.

Optional variations

- substitute bulgar wheat for the quinoa.

- substitute red and green peppers for the apple.

Bolivian squash stew

This is one of many South American recipes for a filling stew which includes those five 'new world' crops which have so enlivened the cooking of the old world - beans, maize, potatoes, squash and tomato. With a crumbly cheese such as Caerphilly added at the last minute, and some wholewheat bread, you have a meal that contains all the elements of a balanced diet as well as one that should satisfy anyone's taste buds.

---

1 kilo (2 lbs) prepared squash
500 g (1lb) potatoes
water
1 onion, chopped
1 large tomato, peeled and chopped
1 tablespoon oil
1/2 teaspoon dried oregano
200 g tin sweetcorn
100 g (4 oz) cooked butter beans
100 g (4 oz) peas
100 g (4 oz) Caerphilly cheese
salt
pepper
2 tablespoons chopped parsley

Chop the squash and potatoes and cover them with cold water. Bring to the boil and simmer for 10 minutes. In a separate pan, fry the onion in the oil until it is soft. Mix this into the squash, then add everything else except the salt, pepper, cheese and parsley.

Cook, stirring gently at intervals, until the squash and potatoes are cooked right through. This should take about 10 - 15 minutes. Taste and season.

Crumble the cheese, stir it in gently and continue to cook until the cheese is beginning to melt. Take the saucepan off the heat, stir in the parsley and transfer the stew to a serving dish.

Jamaican pumpkin and fish stew

In this sweet and sour stew, the fish is added towards the end of the cooking time and sits on top of the other ingredients to cook in the fragrant steam. I've suggested cod here, but you could use any other flakey-fleshed fish, such as haddock or hake.

2 tablespoons corn oil
1 medium onion, chopped
3cm (1") ginger root, grated
500 g (1lb) prepared pumpkin
1 tablespoon Tabasco sauce
2 tablespoons soft brown sugar
1 tablespoon white wine vinegar
water
salt
4 pieces cod, total 500 g (1lb)

In a large saucepan, fry the onion and ginger root in the oil for 5 minutes. Chop the pumpkin into smallish chunks and add it to the saucepan with the Tabasco, sugar and vinegar. Add just enough water to cover, stir gently to mix everything, then place the fish on top.

Bring the liquid up to the boil, then turn down the heat and cover the pan to simmer until the fish is cooked - 20 - 30 minutes.

To serve, use a slotted spoon to lift the fish out onto plates, then add a portion of the stew.

Chinese-style squash and green bean stew

'Chinese-style' is a bit of a misnomer here, as stewing isn't really part of the Chinese way of cooking. But this stew includes black bean sauce and soy sauce, and to be frank, I couldn't think what else to call it!

2 tablespoons oil
2 small onions, finely chopped
1 clove garlic, finely chopped
3cm (1") ginger root, grated
1 teaspoon chilli powder
2 tablespoons black bean sauce
500 g (1 lb) prepared squash
300 ml (1/2 pint) vegetable stock
250 g (8 oz) fresh green beans
2 tablespoons rich soy sauce
1 tablespoon chopped fresh coriander leaves

Heat the oil and fry the onions and garlic until they are translucent. Add the ginger root, chilli powder and black bean sauce and fry gently, stirring, for 3 - 4 minutes.

Chop the squash into fairly small chunks and add them to the saucepan with half the stock. Bring the mixture to the boil and simmer for 10 minutes. Add the green beans and the rest of the stock, bring it back to simmering point and cook until the beans are done - about 5 minutes.

Stir in the soy sauce and serve garnished with the coriander.

Native American squash and turkey stew

Native Americans make a lot of stews, using whatever combinations of meat and vegetables are available. Along the eastern side of North America, wild turkeys were plentiful, and comparatively easy to catch, hence this dish. Before the advent of the mincer, they would have cooked and then shredded the turkey meat, but it's easier to do it this way.

250 g (8 oz) minced raw turkey
1 tablespoon oil
1 medium onion, chopped
1 clove garlic, crushed
$\frac{1}{2}$ teaspoon chilli powder
2 teaspoons tomato purée
250 g (8 oz) prepared squash
water
salt

Brown the turkey in the oil, stirring to separate the grains of meat, then add the onion and garlic and fry gently for 5 minutes. Stir in the chilli powder and tomato purée.

Chop the squash into fairly small chunks and add it to the pan, stirring to mix it well. Add sufficient water to just cover it, bring it to the boil then turn it down to simmer, covered, for 40 - 45 minutes. Taste and season, cook another 5 minutes before serving.

Optional variations

● replace the chilli powder with your preferred strength of curry powder.

● add 1 tablespoon sultanas.

Jamaican lamb stew with squash

I suspect that the meat originally used in this recipe would have been kid rather than lamb. You could use kid if you like, but I find it a bit over-strong for my taste. Choose a lean cut of lamb, or trim off as much fat as you can, give it plenty of time to cook and tenderise, then serve it on a bed of rice.

---

1 kilo (2 lbs) lamb
1 kilo (2 lbs) prepared squash
2 tablespoons oil
3 medium onions, sliced
2 cloves garlic, crushed
1 teaspoon powdered ginger
4 tablespoons curry powder
4 large tomatoes, peeled and chopped
1 1/2 litres (3 pints) vegetable stock or water

Cut the lamb and the squash into 3cm (1") cubes. Set the squash aside, and seal the lamb, in batches, in the oil, removing it once it is sealed.

Fry the onions and garlic in the oil until they are translucent, stir in the powdered ginger and curry powder, then add the lamb and toss it to coat it in the spices. Add the tomatoes and enough of the stock to cover the meat, bring it to the boil and turn it down to a slow simmer.

Cover the pan and let it stew until the meat is nearly tender. This could take up to 2 hours, so you will need to check it at intervals to make sure it isn't sticking. Add more stock as needed.

Taste and season, add the squash cubes, and cook for a further 20 - 30 minutes, until both the squash and the lamb are tender.

Squash goulash with herbed dumplings

This is the sort of meal I like to come home to after working on our allotment on those cold days when you feel you have to tidy up for the winter and get as much digging done as you can before the ground gets too wet to work. I set the stew cooking in my crock-pot before we go out, my husband makes the dumplings while I have a quick soak in the bath to get the kinks out of my back, then I get out of the bath and he climbs in while the dumplings cook and I set the table. Then, as often as not, we eat still wrapped in our bath robes (If we're really starved, we make extra dumplings and finish them off with golden syrup.)

Any of the denser-fleshed squash will do for this recipe, such as Buttercup, Butternut, Hubbard or Kabocha.

1 green pepper, chopped
1 large onion, chopped
2 tablespoons olive oil
2 large potatoes, roughly chopped
500 g (1 lb) squash, roughly chopped
400 g tin chopped tomatoes
1 tablespoon paprika
salt
150 ml (5 fl oz) soured cream

Dumplings

300 g (12 oz) self-raising flour
100 g (4 oz) suet
generous pinch salt
1 teaspoon dried thyme
water

In a large saucepan, fry the pepper and onion in the oil for 2 - 3 minutes. Add the potatoes, squash, tomatoes, salt and paprika, and simmer until the vegetables are tender - about 50 - 60 minutes.

Make the dumplings 20 minutes before you are ready to eat (see page 69). Put all the dry ingredients into a mixing bowl and add sufficient water to make a fairly soft dough. Form this into 8 balls, then cook them for 15 minutes, either in a steamer or in the goulash, having first brought this back to the boil.

Stir the sour cream into the goulash just before serving.

Squash couscous

Couscous is a grain-like staple made from wheat, but it is also a spicy North African stew, served with the couscous which is cooked over the stew. If you don't have an authentic couscousier, you can line a metal colander with butter muslin and stand it on top of a big saucepan, or you can cook the couscous separately in a microwave. You can even get 'quick' couscous which needs no more than to soak in boiling water for 20 minutes. Or you can cheat and use rice instead!

You can use any of the firmer fleshed squash for this recipe, such as Butternut, Buttercup, Hubbard, or Kabocha.

---

250 g (8 oz) couscous or basmati rice
4 tablespoons olive oil
1 onion, sliced thinly
1/2 teaspoon ground turmeric
1/2 teaspoon ground ginger
1/4 teaspoon chilli powder
1 teaspoon ground coriander seed
500 g (1 lb) prepared squash, cubed
250 g (8 oz) carrots, in thick slices
400 g tin chopped tomatoes
400 g tin chick peas, drained
salt
pepper

In a large saucepan, fry the onion in the oil until it has softened. Add the spices and fry 2 - 3 minutes, stirring. Add all the vegetables, season, bring the mixture to the boil, then simmer gently until all the vegetables are tender - about an hour. You may need to add some stock, especially if you are cooking the couscous over the stew.

If not steaming the couscous over the stew, prepare it according to the instructions on the packet. Serve by tipping the couscous onto a large dish, forming a depression in the middle and then tipping the stew into this.

Pumpkin and lentil stew

This is a recipe I first encountered in France, made with the little black Le Puy lentils from the rich volcanic soil of the Auvergne. I am very fond of all the pulses, but these lentils are my favourite - quick to cook, and with a wonderful earthy flavour. Real comfort food.

---

100 g (4 oz) Le Puy lentils
1 bay leaf
3 medium onions, sliced
2 cloves garlic, crushed
2 tablespoons olive oil
500 g (1 lb) prepared pumpkin flesh, in large chunks
6 tomatoes, peeled and chopped
1 teaspoon thyme
1 teaspoon sugar
salt
pepper

Cook the lentils in plenty of boiling water with the bay leaf until they are tender - about 20 minutes. Drain them and throw away the bay leaf.

Gently fry the onions and garlic in the oil until tender. Add the pumpkin and toss it a little to coat it in oil. Add the lentils, tomatoes, thyme and sugar, then season to taste before stewing until the pumpkin is tender and everything is amalgamated.

Savouries and main courses

Squash pasta

Although I'm not totally convinced that plain fresh pasta tastes any better than the dry sort, there are times when you do need to make your own - when you want to make ravioli, for instance, or when you want a special flavour which you can't buy. I put off making pasta for years, but of course I had to try it when I started testing recipes for this book, and was delighted to find that it really is perfectly easy. And with a good-flavoured squash included in the ingredients, the end product really is worth the little bit of effort involved in kneading and rolling the dough.

Do take the trouble to get proper pasta flour though, as it gives a far better result than ordinary plain flour. As with squash bread, it is best to use a fairly dry-fleshed variety of squash such as Buttercup or Crown Prince.

---

550 g (18 oz) pasta flour
250 g (8 oz) squash purée
1 large egg
1 teaspoon olive oil
4 - 6 tablespoons water

Mix the squash purée into 500 g (1 lb) of the flour until it resembles fine breadcrumbs. This can be done in a food processor. Add the egg and oil and the water (a tablespoonful at a time) and mix to a firm dough.

Sprinkle some of the remaining flour on your work-surface and knead the dough for 10 minutes until it is smooth. Cover it with a clean tea-towel and let it rest for 30 minutes.

Roll it out by hand or in a pasta roller as thin as possible. For ravioli, leave it to rest in the sheet and add your fillings as normal. For fettucine, roll it up and cut slices off the end, then shake these out and leave them to rest for a further 10 minutes before cooking them in plenty of salted boiling water.

To enjoy the delicate flavour of this pasta, serve it with a simple sauce, or just butter and Parmesan cheese, or use it to accompany a meat dish such as veal or chicken. Alternatively, try it with apricot cream sauce as a sweet (page 117).

Pumpkin ravioli

Using pumpkin or squash to stuff ravioli has become one of the 'standards' of Italian peasant cooking, but I find the basic version rather too bland for my taste. So I experimented a little and came up with this sharper version, using sun-dried tomatoes and chilli peppers.

If you fancy the filling, but don't want to make your own pasta, you can use wonton wrappers instead.

Pasta

550 g (18 oz) pasta flour
1 large egg
1 teaspoon olive oil
6 - 8 tablespoons water

Add the egg and the oil to the flour and mix to a firm dough, adding the water a tablespoonful at a time.

Sprinkle some of the remaining flour on your work-surface and knead the dough for 10 minutes until it is smooth. Cover it with a clean tea-towel and let it rest for 30 minutes.

Roll it out by hand or in a pasta roller as thin as possible. Leave it to rest for 10 minutes while you mix the filling.

Filling

250 g (8 oz) pumpkin or squash purée
4 - 6 sun-dried tomatoes, finely chopped
1 small green chilli pepper, de-seeded and finely chopped

Mix the filling ingredients thoroughly.

The 'official' method of making ravioli is to cut the pasta into two sheets, dot the filling on one of them, then cover it with the other. I find this rather tricky, so I do it this way: Decide how big you want your ravioli to be - 5cm (2") is a reasonable size - then mark the sheet of pasta in strips. Don't cut right through, just make a guiding mark. Then ignore the outside strip and dot the filling at intervals down the middle of the next strip. (A 5cm (2") ravioli will need a teaspoon of filling.)

Moisten the pasta round each blob of filling with a little water, then fold the outside strip over to cover the filling and press it down with the heel of your hand. Avoid leaving air space inside the individual ravioli. Cut this strip of ravioli off the sheet and repeat the operation.

If using wonton wrappers you can either use two wrappers to make one big ravioli, or fold each sheet diagonally to make a triangular ravioli, or make two smaller ravioli from each wrapper.

Bring a large saucepan of salted water to the boil, and slip the ravioli in, taking care that they do not stick to each other, and cook them at a fast rolling boil for 4 - 5 minutes. Drain well before serving.

Optional variations

- add 1 - 2 tablespoons chopped fresh sage to the pasta dough mixture.
- omit the tomato and chilli from the filling, replacing it with up to 100 g (4 oz) finely minced chicken breast.
- omit the tomatoes and chilli, replacing them with 1 tablespoon of finely chopped Mostarda (Italian fruits preserved with mustard).
- omit the chilli and put a small cube of Mozarella cheese in each ravioli with the filling.
- omit the tomato and chilli and replace it with 100 g (4 oz) button mushrooms, chopped and fried in a little butter.
- use half the given quantity of squash and add an equal amount of haricot beans, cooked and mashed.

Squash pasta ravioli with Ricotta and spinach filling

Because the flavour of squash pasta is so delicate, it would be a pity to swamp that flavour with a strong-tasting filling. So this Ricotta and spinach filling is ideal. Serve it with a sprinkle of either a good-flavoured estate bottled olive oil, or walnut oil and a generous grind of black pepper.

---

250 g (8 oz) cooked chopped spinach
250 g (8 oz) Ricotta cheese
1 recipe squash pasta (page 37)
2 tablespoons olive or walnut oil
black pepper

Squeeze any excess moisture from the spinach and mix it well with the Ricotta cheese. Roll out the pasta to a thin sheet then let it rest for 10 minutes before filling in the normal way (see page 37).

Bring a large saucepan of salted water to the boil, and slip the ravioli in, taking care that they do not stick to each other, and cook them at a fast rolling boil for 4 - 5 minutes. Drain well before serving. Pass the oil and pepper for diners to add as they wish.

Optional variations

- add 50 g (2 oz) finely chopped walnuts to the filling.
- sprinkle chopped fresh dill leaves on top when serving.

Baked pumpkin gnocchi

Gnocchi is little more than large pieces of pasta dough, cooked in boiling water. It can either be served with a sauce, just like pasta, or it and its sauce can be put in a gratin dish and baked. Often the sauce will be cheese-based, but this one is a thin pesto made with rosemary and almonds, echoing the nuts which enhance the pasta dough itself.

Gnocchi

250 g (8 oz) squash purée
550 g (18 oz) pasta flour
50 g (2 oz) ground almonds
1 large egg
1 teaspoon olive oil
4 - 6 tablespoons water

Sauce

2 tablespoons chopped rosemary
2 cloves garlic, coarsely chopped
250 ml (8 fl oz) olive oil
75 g (3 oz) grated Parmesan cheese
1 tablespoon flaked almonds

Mix the squash purée into 500 g (1 lb) of the flour until it resembles fine breadcrumbs. This can be done in a food processor. Add the ground almond, egg and oil and the water (a tablespoonful at a time) and knead to a soft dough.

Roll the dough into sausages, then cut off pieces about 4cm (1 ½") long. If you like, you can roll these against the tines of a fork to create ridges.

Bring a saucepan of salted water to the boil and slide in the gnocchi. Simmer them until they float to the surface - about 5 minutes. Drain well.

Meanwhile, preheat the oven to 375°F (190°C) Gas Mark 5 and butter a gratin dish.

Put all the sauce ingredients except the flaked almonds into a food processor and whizz them to a thin paste.

Stand the gnocchi upright in the gratin dish and pour the sauce over them. Sprinkle the flaked almonds on top and bake for 25 minutes.

Pasta with squash sauces

There are a number of ways you can enjoy pasta with the addition of squash or pumpkin flesh. Here are a few of them for you to try. For the soft purée-like sauces, choose spaghetti or tagliatelle; for the thicker sauces, choose one of the large shapes such as conchiglie which will hold the bigger pieces.

Any of these sauces, made a bit thicker, would make good stuffings for ravioli.

Butternut, aubergine and apple with pasta

1 large aubergine
1 cooking apple, preferably Bramley, peeled and cored
the bell end of a Butternut squash, prepared
1 egg, beaten
2 tablespoons plain flour
2 cloves garlic
olive oil for frying
500 g (1 lb) dried pasta - ideally conchiglie
black pepper
grated Parmesan cheese

Cut the aubergine, apple and squash into small cubes. Toss them first in the egg, then the flour. Halve the garlic cloves and fry them briefly in the oil, then remove and discard them. Put the vegetables in the oil and stir-fry them until tender.

Cook and drain your pasta, then toss the vegetables with the pasta before serving it with a generous grind of black pepper, and Parmesan sprinkled on top.

Pasta with pumpkin and red pepper sauce

1 medium onion, chopped finely
1 red pepper, chopped finely
25 g (1 oz) butter
250 g (8 oz) pumpkin purée
90 ml (3 fl oz) milk
salt
pepper
120 ml (4 fl oz) single cream
500 g (1 lb) dried pasta - spaghetti, tagliatelle,
fusilli or fettucine

Sauté the onion and pepper in the butter until they are soft. Stir in the pumpkin purée and the milk and heat through. Taste and season before lowering the heat and stirring in the cream. Heat through gently.

Cook and drain your pasta, then toss it with the sauce before serving.

Pasta with squash, Feta cheese, spinach and garlic

2 - 6 cloves garlic to taste
4 tablespoons olive oil
100 g (4 oz) frozen chopped spinach, thawed to room
   temperature
100 g (4 oz) squash purée (ideally Buttercup
   or Crown Prince)
75 g (3 oz) Feta cheese, mashed
500 g (1 lb) dried pasta - spaghetti, tagliatelle, fusilli
   or fettucine

Crush or finely chop the garlic cloves and fry them gently in the oil until they are soft. Add the spinach and toss it for 3 - 4 minutes. Add the squash purée and the mashed Feta cheese, cook, stirring until it is all warmed through.

Cook and drain your pasta then toss it with the sauce before serving.

Squash risotto (p52)

Very rich squash and blue cheese sauce

50 g (2 oz) butter
2 cloves garlic, crushed
250 g (8 oz) squash, prepared and grated (Butternut
    or Kabocha would be good)
150 ml (5 fl oz) double cream
100 g (4 oz) Dolcelatte cheese
100 g (4 oz) Mascarpone cheese
salt
pepper
2 leaves fresh sage, chopped
nutmeg
500 g (1 lb) dried pasta - spaghetti, tagliatelle, fusilli
    or fettucine

In a large frying pan, fry the garlic in the butter for a couple of minutes, then add the grated squash. Cook, stirring, 5 minutes until the squash is tender. Stir in the cream and cook until it is hot.

Cut the cheeses into small pieces and add them to the sauce, stirring until the cheese has softened and incorporated itself with the pumpkin. Taste and season.

Cook and drain your pasta then toss it with the sauce before sprinkling on the sage and a generous grating of nutmeg to serve.

Red Camargue rice stuffing in Acorn squash (p56)

Squash lasagne or cannelloni

This is a variation on the usual vegetarian lasagne recipes, which rely on aubergine or mushrooms for their 'meaty' layer. Not that I have anything against either of those, but sometimes I feel like a change, so I experimented a bit and came up with this. I didn't want to swamp the squash taste with tomato, so to provide a contrast to what might otherwise be rather bland flavours, I used yoghurt in the squash layers and fennel in the cheesey layers.

You can either make it in layers, like the usual lasagne, or roll the pasta sheets up to make cannelloni, putting the squash mixture inside and the cheese mixture over the top before you bake it. Either way, all it needs to go with it is a green salad of rocket, or of mixed leaves which includes chicory.

---

8 sheets lasagne
500 g (1 lb) squash
75 g (3 oz) walnuts, chopped
500 g pot yoghurt
50 g (2 oz) butter
2 bulbs fennel
1 tablespoon plain flour
salt
pepper
100 g (4 oz) Gruyère cheese, grated
100 g (4 oz) Mozarella cheese, sliced thinly

Preheat the oven to 375°F (190°C) Gas Mark 5 and grease a large baking dish.

Cook the sheets of lasagne in a large saucepan of boiling salted water until they are *al dente* - about 6 minutes. If making cannelloni, cut them into suitable rectangles.

Cut the squash flesh into small cubes and steam them briefly. (You could do this over the water in which the lasagne cooks.) Drain and mix with one third of the yoghurt and the walnuts.

Trim the fennel, remove the tender centres and save these to add to the salad. Chop the rest into fairly small chunks. Cook these gently in the butter until they are tender. Stir in the flour and cook for 2 minutes, then gradually add the rest of the yoghurt. If it threatens to separate, add a little more flour. Finally add the Gruyère and continue stirring until this has melted into the sauce. Remove from the heat.

Assemble the dish. For lasagne, start with a layer of squash mixture, then a layer of pasta, then a layer of cheese sauce, and repeat, ending with a layer of cheese sauce.

For cannelloni, spread 2 tablespoonsful of cheese sauce over the bottom of the dish. Lay the strips of pasta on the work surface and divide the squash mixture between the strips, then roll up each strip before laying it in the dish with the join downwards. Pour the rest of the cheese sauce over the top of the dish.

Lay the Mozarella slices on top of the dish, and bake it for 35 - 40 minutes.

Squash dough pizza

My preference in pizzas is for the deep-pan variety, with a turned-up lip that allows me to pile on lots of topping. The first time I made squash focaccia and saw how the crust browned, I realised that this was the perfect dough for pizza, so I made another batch, rolled it out thin and reached for the tomato sauce and Mozarella.

One recipe squash focaccia (page 89) makes two large pizza bases, so you can either use half the quantities, or freeze the second piece for another time.

---

1 recipe squash focaccia
1 - 2 tablespoons olive oil
250 g bottle tomato sauce or pizza topping
100 g (4 oz) Gruyère or Cheddar cheese, grated
100 g (4 oz) Mozarella cheese, sliced thin
1 teaspoon dried thyme or rosemary

plus as many of the following as you like or feel inclined to add:

red and green peppers, sliced into rings
onion, thinly sliced
streaky bacon or ham, cut into strips
beefsteak tomato, sliced
pine nuts
black olives
anchovies
fresh mushrooms, thinly sliced

Make the dough according to the recipe on page 89, and proceed to the second rise stage. Instead of putting the dough into a baking tin, divide it in two and use the heel of your hand to press each piece out into a flat round about 1cm ($1/2$") thick, leaving the edges a little thicker than the centre.

Preheat the oven to 425°F (220°C) Gas Mark 7. Lightly flour a baking tray or pizza 'brick'.

Paint the outside edge of the bases with the olive oil before spreading the tomato topping over the centre. Sprinkle the Gruyère or Cheddar cheese over the topping. Add whatever else you like, ending with the slices of Mozarella and a sprinkle of herbs.

Bake for about 20 minutes, until the base is golden-brown and the toppings are all nicely melted together.

Spaghetti squash - basic

Spaghetti squash has a delicate but definite flavour, and can be eaten cold as a salad, hot with dressings, or can be treated as though it were real spaghetti. For anyone who wants to avoid the calories and carbohydrates in pasta, spaghetti squash is a good substitute. A medium-sized squash weighing about 1 kilo (2 lbs) should be enough for 2 people. See page 12 for preparation details.

To enjoy it cold, dress it with a vinaigrette dressing, a rémoulade dressing of mustard flavoured mayonnaise, or the Japanese-style dressing below.

To enjoy it hot as an accompaniment for meat dishes, dress it with a little salt, a generous grating of nutmeg and 2 tablespoons olive or nut oil. When serving it with fish or chicken, add 1 teaspoon of lemon zest.

Japanese-style dressing for cold spaghetti squash

> **1 tablespoon balsamic vinegar**
> **1 tablespoon red wine vinegar**
> **1 tablespoon sesame oil**
> **1 tablespoon peanut oil**
> **1 red pepper, chopped finely**
> **1 fresh red chilli pepper, chopped finely (optional)**
> **7cm (3") ginger root**
> **10 nasturtium leaves, chopped**
> **2 tablespoons toasted sesame seeds**

Grate the ginger root into a piece of butter muslin. Pick up the edges of the muslin to form a little bag and wring it tightly to extract as much juice as you can. Add this juice to the rest of the ingredients and whisk them together before pouring them over the strands of squash. Toss well and serve straight away.

Spaghetti squash primavera

This is no more than a variation on the classic pasta primavera, given a new dimension through the lighter texture and delicate flavour of the squash. I've listed 10 different vegetables in the list of ingredients but you do not have to use all of them. The idea is to use contrasting colours and shapes to make the dish look really attractive, and as its name implies, it is a spring-time dish when the new season's vegetables are available, so use small specimens or chop larger ones into small pieces.

Cooked flesh from 2 medium spaghetti squash
1 kilo (2 lbs) of vegetables made up of:
small florets of broccoli
fresh peas
baby carrots
asparagus tips
snap peas
spring onions
baby turnips
baby courgettes
red, green or gold peppers
button mushrooms, thinly sliced
500 ml (16 fl oz) single cream
120 ml (4 fl oz) light stock
1 tablespoon Dijon mustard
4 tablespoons grated Parmesan cheese
2 tablespoons chopped fresh herbs

Cook the squash, drain them and take out the flesh, separating the strands.

Prepare the vegetables. If using mushrooms, fry them lightly in butter. Steam the other vegetables until just tender.

In a large saucepan, warm the cream, stock and mustard together, stirring gently so that the cream does not separate. Add the squash and vegetables, tossing well to cover with the sauce. Turn out into a serving dish, sprinkle over the Parmesan and chopped herbs and toss again gently before serving.

Spaghetti squash with cheese and nuts

This simple way of dressing spaghetti squash makes a light supper dish, served with a salad of mixed green leaves and some good brown bread. You don't have to add the nuts, but they do add another textural dimension to the soft strands of squash.

---

25 g (1 oz) unsalted butter
3 - 4 cloves garlic, crushed
2 medium sized spaghetti squash, each weighing about
    1 kilo (2 lbs)
50 g (2 oz) Dolcelatte cheese, in small chunks
50 g (2 oz) toasted hazlenuts, chopped
2 leaves of sage, chopped
50 g (2 oz) grated Parmesan cheese
salt
pepper

Melt the butter and fry the garlic for 2 - 3 minutes, then remove the garlic.

Cook the squash and extract the strands of flesh. Pour the butter over it, add the Dolcelatte, hazelnuts and sage. Toss well, season and serve with the Parmesan sprinkled on top.

Optional variations

- substitute chopped walnut for the hazelnuts.
- add 50 g (2 oz) finely sliced button mushrooms.

Spaghetti squash with watercress cream

This dish is more suited to serving as a starter than as a main course or accompaniment, so I've only listed a single squash. If you want more, just double up on everything, or double up on the sauce ingredients and add 100 g (4 oz) vermicelli to add a little bulk.

---

1 bunch watercress
4 tablespoons thick yoghurt
50 g (2 oz) butter
3 tablespoons white wine vinegar
1 spaghetti squash
pepper

Save a couple of sprigs of watercress for garnishing, and whizz the rest in a food processor or liquidizer with the yoghurt.

In a small saucepan, melt the butter then whisk into it the vinegar. Keep whisking until the mixture emulsifies into a cream-like consistency.

Meanwhile, cook the squash, drain it and fork out the strands. Toss them in the butter and vinegar mixture, then in the watercress cream. Sprinkle with a generous grinding of pepper and garnish with the remaining watercress to serve.

Stuffed spaghetti squash

This is a variation on the spaghetti squash theme, in that you prepare everything, then put it back in the shell to bake. If you wish, you can prepare it ahead of time and give it a little longer in the oven to warm it through as well as melt the cheese.

---

2 medium spaghetti squash
150 g (6 oz) Mozarella cheese
50 g (2 oz) Parmesan cheese, grated
250 g (8 oz) Ricotta cheese
1/2 teaspoon marjoram
1/2 teaspoon thyme
300 ml (1/2 pint) tomato sauce or passata
salt
pepper

Cook and drain the spaghetti squash in the usual way, then cut them open carefully lengthwise. Scrape out and throw away the seeds, then carefully scrape out the strands of flesh, retaining the skins.

Cut a third of the Mozarella cheese into thin slices and retain these. Grate or finely chop the rest and mix it with the Parmesan and Ricotta. Mix in the herbs, pepper and tomato sauce, then toss the strands of squash in this sauce before packing it into the squash skins. Fit these into a baking pan.

When you are ready to cook the squash, preheat the oven to 350°F (180°C) Gas Mark 4. Pour boiling water into the baking pan to come about 10cm (4") up the sides of the squash. Arrange the slices of Mozarella on top of the squash.

If cooking from cold, bake for 25 minutes, otherwise for 15 minutes, until the Mozarella has melted.

Winter squash pie

Serves 6

This succulent pie is a firm favourite in France, where it is sold from stalls in markets and at the increasingly popular pumpkin fairs. It makes a main course for a vegetarian meal, or a tasty lunch or supper dish for anyone who enjoys their vegetables. Eaten cold, it makes a tasty addition to a picnic. For this recipe, use any of the dense fleshed winter squashes, such as Buttercup, Butternut, Hubbard or Kabocha. If you can't get the dense-fleshed varieties, degorge the flesh before cooking it.

---

500 g (1 lb) shortcrust pastry
500 g (1 lb) winter squash purée
6 shallots or small onions, finely chopped
1 small bunch of flat-leaved parsley, chopped
1 egg, beaten
1/2 teaspoon ground cinnamon
salt
black pepper
egg yolk or milk for brushing the pastry
60 ml (2 fl oz) single cream

Pre-heat the oven to 400°F (200°C) Gas Mark 6.

Meanwhile, roll out the pastry and use two thirds of it to line a medium size pie dish, leaving about 3cm (1") of pastry to hang over the edges of the dish. Save the rest for the lid.

Mash the shallots and the parsley into the squash with the egg and cinnamon. Season to taste. Spread the mash into the lined pie dish and add the lid, folding the spare pastry over the top of the lid.

Brush the top of the pie with egg yolk or milk and bake for 30 - 40 minutes, until the top is golden-brown.

Just before serving, cut carefully round the lid at the edge of the folded pastry, lift this section off and pour in the cream before replacing the lid. Serve hot with a selection of steamed vegetables or a thick tomato sauce, or cold with a salad or on its own.

Optional variations

- omit the cinnamon and add a teaspoon of dried sage or 2 leaves, chopped, of fresh sage.
- add 50 - 100 g (2 - 4 oz) cooked ham and/or wild mushrooms.

Squash risotto

Quite apart from the fact that I like the taste of risotto, it's one of the dishes that I find soothing to prepare at the end of a busy day. There's nothing like standing at the stove, stirring gently and adding this and that, to help you wind down.

If you want to serve this risotto for a dinner party, you could use the shell of the squash as a serving bowl, choosing a green skinned squash to provide a contrast from the gold of the contents. (See page 13 for instructions on preparing the shell.)

---

100 g (4 oz) butter
1 medium onion, chopped
2 cloves garlic, finely chopped
500 g (1 lb) prepared winter squash
300 g (12 oz) arborio rice
2 leaves of fresh sage, chopped, or $\frac{1}{2}$ teaspoon dried sage
salt
pepper
120 ml (4 fl oz) medium sherry
900 ml (1 $\frac{1}{2}$ pints) chicken or vegetable stock, heated
50 g (2 oz) grated Parmesan cheese

Cut the squash into smallish chunks*.

Melt half the butter and fry the onion until it is translucent. Add the garlic, then the chunks of squash, stir well and cook for 2 minutes. Add the rice and sage, and cook for 2 minutes, stirring. Season.

Add the sherry, stirring until it is absorbed. Add a ladleful of stock and stir until it is absorbed. Continue doing this until the rice is cooked, adding the stock a ladleful at a time. You may not need all the stock. The rice should be *al dente* rather than soggy, but the texture of the risotto should be moist rather than dry.

Stir in the rest of the butter and the Parmesan cheese before serving with more Parmesan for those who want it.

*If you want the squash to break down during cooking, choose Kabocha or Onion squash and cut it into 5mm ($\frac{1}{4}$ ") chunks. If you prefer the squash to stay in chunks, choose Butternut, Buttercup or Hubbard squash and cut it into 10mm ($\frac{1}{2}$ ") chunks.

Optional variations

● use rosemary instead of sage leaves.

● add 25 g (1 oz) shelled pistachio nuts.

Punjabi spiced pumpkin

You can make curried pumpkin, as you can any other form of curry, by using purchased curry powder or paste, but it always tastes better if you use the individual spices. You can buy the chilli powder, cumin seeds and turmeric easily enough from supermarkets, but you will probably need to go to an Indian grocer for the mango powder and nigella seeds. The secret with all spices is to buy them in small quantities so they don't go stale before you use them up.

> **2 tablespoons vegetable oil**
> **1 level teaspoon cumin seeds**
> **1/4 teaspoon nigella seeds**
> **2 medium onions, thinly sliced**
> **3cm (1") piece of fresh ginger root, thinly sliced**
> **1/4 level teaspoon chilli powder**
> **1/2 level teaspoon turmeric powder**
> **1 teaspoon salt**
> **500 g (1 lb) prepared pumpkin in 3cm (1") chunks**
> **2 ripe tomatoes, chopped**
> **300 ml (1/2 pint) water**
> **2 level teaspoons mango powder**

Heat the oil over a high heat, add the cumin and nigella seeds and stir them until they start to pop. Reduce the heat, add the onions and ginger root and fry until the onions are golden. Add the chilli powder, turmeric and salt, and fry for 1 minute.

Add the tomatoes and pumpkin chunks, stir well to coat them with the spices, then add the water, bring it to the boil then cover the saucepan and simmer for about 20 minutes, until the pumpkin is tender.

Stir in the mango powder, cook for 4 - 5 minutes, then serve with rice, poppadums and another vegetable curry if you like.

Optional variation

● add a tin of chick peas, drained, and a large sliced banana.

Squash and celeriac crumble

Celeriac is an ugly-looking vegetable, but it has all the flavour of celery without the high water content. Just be careful when peeling it that you drop each piece into water straight away, as otherwise it tends to discolour. It marries well with squash, giving a white contrast that increases the 'eye-appeal' of this dish. Butternut squash is ideal, or one of the other golden-fleshed varieties.

---

250 g (8 oz) prepared squash
250 g (8 oz) prepared celeriac
50 g (2 oz) butter
2 small onions, chopped
5 rashers streaky bacon, chopped
1 tablespoon plain flour
400 ml (15 fl oz) milk
salt
white pepper
3 thick slices white or brown bread, crumbed
75 g (3 oz) Cheddar cheese, grated

Preheat the oven to 325°F (160°C) Gas Mark 3 and butter a gratin dish.

Cut the squash and celeriac into similar sized and shaped pieces, then steam them together until they are tender. Celeriac takes a little longer to cook than squash, so for this recipe you will need to slice it more thinly than the squash, or put it in the steamer first, to start cooking while you chop the squash.

Meanwhile, melt the butter in a saucepan and fry the onion and bacon for 5 minutes. Stir in the flour to make a roux. Then gradually add the milk, stirring constantly. Season. Tip the vegetables into the gratin dish and pour the sauce over them. Mix the breadcrumbs and grated cheese together and sprinkle this over the top of the sauce.

If you've worked fast enough for the vegetables and the sauce to be hot when you put the dish in the oven, bake for 20 minutes, until the top is golden brown. If you've prepared the dish in advance or it is cold when it goes into the oven, it will need another 5 - 10 minutes to heat through thoroughly as well as brown the top.

Optional variations

• add 50 g (2 oz) pine nuts or chopped walnuts to the crumble mix.

Pumpkin filled with corn and cream

This is a dish for those times when you need something rich and creamy in your mouth, and don't care about the effect on your waistline. Almost fondue like in texture, you could make it the centre-piece of an informal supper for friends, taking it in turns to dip a piece of bread into the depths, then spooning out the residue onto separate plates.

---

1 medium sized pumpkin, about 1 kilo (2 lbs) in weight
200 g tin creamed sweetcorn
100 g (4 oz) Gruyère cheese, grated
120 ml (4 fl oz) single cream
salt
pepper
nutmeg, grated

Preheat the oven to 375°F (190°C) Gas Mark 5.

Cut a lid in the pumpkin and remove the seeds, then remove enough flesh to make a good-sized hollow.

Drain the corn and tip it into the pumpkin, adding a sprinkle of salt and pepper. Tip in the cheese and another sprinkle of salt and pepper. Finally, pour in the cream to within 3cm (1") of the top and season again, ending with a sprinkle of nutmeg.

Put the 'lid' back on the pumpkin, stand it in an oven-proof dish and cover the whole thing with foil. Bake it for 20 - 30 minutes, until a skewer inserted into the top of the pumpkin penetrates easily.

Remove the foil, take off the lid, stir the contents gently, add more seasoning and nutmeg, and replace the lid before taking it to the table. Scrape some of the pumpkin flesh out as you serve it, but be careful not to pierce the skin below the liquid level.

Red Camargue rice stuffing for Acorn squash

This red rice is a new discovery, currently grown only on one farm in the Camargue where it quietly hybridized itself when no-one was looking.

The flavour is really nutty, and the texture when cooked is rather like brown rice, but it does not go mushy as brown rice can. Finally, it's an attractive reddish brown colour, which contrasts well with the gold of the squash and the red and green of the sweet peppers. I've suggested Acorn squash here, but any of the small varieties such as Gold Nugget or Sweet Dumpling could be substituted.

---

200 g (8 oz) red Camargue rice
100 g (4 oz) raisins
2 tablespoons olive oil
1 medium onion, thinly sliced
1 small red pepper, chopped
1 small green pepper, chopped
50 g (2 oz) pine nuts
pepper
4 Acorn squash, prepared for stuffing

Preheat the oven to 400°F (200°C) Gas Mark 6.

Cook the rice in plenty of boiling salted water for 30 minutes, then take it off the heat and leave it to stand for another 20 minutes before rinsing and draining it. Meanwhile, pour boiling water over the raisins and leave them to plump up for 30 minutes before draining them.

In a large frying pan or a wok, heat the oil and fry the peppers and onion until the onion is translucent. Add the drained rice and toss the mixture for a couple of minutes. Add the drained raisins, the pine nuts and pepper to your taste, and toss the mixture well.

Spoon the rice mixture into the squashes, and stand them in a roasting pan. Pour 3cm (1") boiling water into the pan, cover the whole thing with foil and bake for 45 minutes.

Serve one squash to each diner, with a crisp salad and some good bread.

Baked fennel with squash and lentil stuffing

Here's an elegant vegetarian supper, with stuffed fennel laid out on a bed of rice. Although it is tasty, some people might find it rather bland, in which case you'll want to add some crisply fried onion as a garnish, or serve some sharp chutney alongside it.

350 g (12 oz) basmati rice
250 g (8 oz) green or red lentils
4 large bulbs of fennel, all the same shape and size
4 tablespoons olive oil
1 teaspoon fennel seeds
1 medium onion, diced
250 g (8 oz) coarse squash purée
salt
pepper

Preheat the oven to 400°F (200°C) Gas Mark 6 and grease a baking dish.

Cook the rice and lentils separately in your usual way.

Trim the fennel by slicing off the base and removing any unsightly outer leaves, then carefully pull off 8 more boat-shaped leaves. These are the containers for the stuffing, so trim the tips a little to make them even. Blanch them in salted boiling water for 3 - 4 minutes, then drain and leave them to cool. Set 3 of the fennel centres aside for another dish, and chop the fourth finely.

Heat the oil and fry the fennel seeds for 3 - 4 minutes, then add the chopped fennel and onion and fry this mixture for another 4 - 5 minutes, until the onion is translucent. Mix in the cooked lentils and squash purée, add salt and pepper to your taste, then spoon the mixture into the fennel 'boats'.

Spread the cooked rice in the baking dish and lay the stuffed fennel boats on top. Cover the whole dish with foil and bake it for 25 minutes.

Serve with crispy fried onions or a sharp chutney.

Squash roulade

Roulades look very impressive, yet they are very easy to make. This one looks best if you use one of the dense golden fleshed squash such as Crown Prince or Hubbard, but it will taste just as good if you use a paler squash such as Butternut. Serve it garnished with a few sprigs of watercress as an elegant starter to dinner, or as a light supper dish with plenty of green salad.

---

3 eggs, separated
500 g (1 lb) squash purée
pinch ground allspice
50 g (2 oz) Gruyère cheese, grated
salt
1 teaspoon sesame seeds

Filling

---

250 g (4 oz) fromage frais
50 g (2 oz) walnut pieces, chopped quite small
2 tablespoons coarsely chopped fresh herbs

Preheat the oven to 400°F (200°C) Gas Mark 6. Line a Swiss roll tin with baking parchment, and cut another sheet of parchment, larger than the tin, for turning the roulade out. Dampen a clean tea-cloth and wring it out well.

Beat the egg whites to soft peaks. Mix the egg yolks, squash purée, allspice, cheese and salt thoroughly, then gently fold in the egg whites.

Pour the mixture into the prepared tin and smooth it into the corners evenly. Sprinkle the sesame seeds on top. Bake it for 15 - 20 minutes, until it feels firm to the touch. Take it out of the oven and leave it in its tin for a couple of minutes, then put the spare sheet of parchment over the top and turn it out onto this. Put the tin aside and carefully peel off the parchment it was baked in. Lay the damp tea-cloth over the top and leave it to cool.

Stir the chopped nuts and herbs into the fromage frais, then spread this over the roulade with a palette knife. Using the parchment it is resting on to help you, roll up the roulade and set it on a serving dish, with the join underneath. Cut slices with a sharp knife to serve.

Savoury squash 'cake'

This is another of those recipes which you look at and think "What an odd lot of ingredients - I don't see how that would work". I thought just that when I encountered the idea for the first time, but I plucked up the courage to try it, and I can assure you that it works very well. It is nice hot or cold, and makes a good central dish for a picnic.

Use any of the dry-fleshed squash, such as Buttercup, Crown Prince, Hubbard or Kabocha.

---

100 g (4 oz) chopped bacon
30 ml (1 fl oz) dry sherry or white wine
75 ml (2¹/₂ fl oz) olive oil
2 eggs
100 g (4 oz) squash purée
50 g (2 oz) grated Cheddar cheese
50 g (2 oz) self raising flour
¹/₂ teaspoon dried active or 'easy blend' yeast
pinch salt
8 black olives, destoned and chopped

Preheat the oven to 375°F (190°C) Gas Mark 5. Prepare a shallow 23cm (9") cake tin or flan tin by buttering and flouring it.

Fry the bacon quickly in its own fat and set it aside to drain.

Mix the sherry and oil, then beat the eggs into it, one at a time. Add the rest of the ingredients and mix well. Pour the mixture into the cake tin and bake it for 25 - 30 minutes, until a skewer comes out clean.

Stand the tin on a wire rack to cool for 10 minutes or so before turning the cake out. Serve slices hot or cold with a salad.

Winter squash gratin

I love gratins and I also love parsnips, so this winter gratin combines the best of both worlds for me. I've given you instructions here to make a white sauce from scratch, but if you have any left over from a previous dish, you could use that, for instance, on one occasion I used parsley sauce and that worked very well.

1 large carrot, roughly chopped
1 medium parsnip, roughly chopped
1 medium leek, roughly chopped
500 g (1 lb) prepared squash chunks
150 ml (5 fl oz) milk
150 ml (5 fl oz) vegetable stock
25 g (1 oz) butter
2 tablespoons plain flour
1 thick slice of bread, crumbed
50 g (2 oz) Gruyère cheese, grated
nutmeg
paprika

Pre-heat the oven to 400°F (200°C) Gas Mark 6 and butter a gratin dish.

Put all the vegetables in a saucepan with the milk and stock, bring it to the boil and simmer until the vegetables are tender - about 15 minutes. Strain them over a bowl, retaining the milk and stock liquid, and turn the vegetables into the buttered gratin dish.

In the same saucepan, melt the butter and stir in the flour to make a roux. Then gradually add the milk and stock mixture, stirring constantly, to make a white sauce. Season and pour over the vegetables.

Mix the breadcrumbs and grated cheese and spread these over the top, then add a sprinkle of nutmeg and a generous sprinkle of paprika.

Bake for 15 minutes, until the top is golden brown and serve with a crisp salad or some good brown bread. If you've worked fast enough for the vegetables and the stock to be hot when you put the dish in the oven, 15 minutes should be sufficient, but if you've prepared the dish in advance or it is cold when it goes into the oven, it will need another 5 - 10 minutes to heat through thoroughly as well as brown the top.

Optional variations

- add 2 sticks of celery or 50 g (2 oz) chestnuts to the vegetables.
- add a handful of chopped parsley to the white sauce.
- add 50 g (2 oz) pumpkin seeds to the topping.

Winter squash, ham and leek gratin

The idea for this dish came from one of those wonderful meals you get in French lorry-drivers restaurants - the Relais Routiers. We were dashing back home from the south and stopped for lunch on the N76 north of Bourges, where we ate a wonderful dish of ham wrapped round sections of leek, under a light cheese sauce. I cooked it a couple of times after we got home, then it occured to me that some squash wouldn't be a bad addition. So I tried it and sure enough, it was good.

2 large Butternut squashes
2 or 3 fat long leeks
8 circular slices of ham
50 g (2 oz) butter
1 tablespoon plain flour
1 teaspoon dry mustard powder
450 ml (³/4 pint) milk
75 g (3 oz) Caerphilly cheese, grated
salt
white pepper

Cut the bell ends off the squash and put them aside for another dish. Peel the straight pieces and cut the flesh of each squash into 4 sticks, just slightly shorter than the diameter of the slices of ham. Trim and clean the leeks, removing the inedible outer leaves, then cut the leeks into sticks the same length as the squash sticks. Take off enough of the next layers of leek leaves to wrap 2 pieces round each squash stick and set the rest aside for another dish.

Wrap the leek round the squash and either steam them for 8 - 10 minutes, or microwave them on high for 4 - 5 minutes, until they are just tender. Let them cool enough to handle, and wrap a slice of ham round each stick. Put 2 sticks on each diner's plate.

Meanwhile, melt the butter in a saucepan and stir in the flour and mustard to make a roux. Then gradually add the milk, stirring constantly, to make a thin white sauce. Then add the cheese and continue stirring until it has melted into the sauce. If it seems too thick, add some more milk. Season.

Spoon the sauce over the wrapped sticks on the plates and pop each plate under the grill for long enough to brown the sauce before serving.

Alternatively, if you want to make this dish in advance, put the sticks and sauce in a gratin dish, then when you are preparing the meal, bake this in a medium oven for about 20 minutes to heat through and brown the top.

Squash gratin

There isn't really a lot of difference between a simple squash gratin and the baked version of a squash purée, other than the texture. However, gratins usually have a lot more sauce, and unlike the purées which are meant to be a side-dish, they can be eaten as a supper or lunch dish with no more than a salad and some good bread (and perhaps a glass of wine).

---

500 g (1 lb) prepared squash, cut into thick slices
 or medium sized chunks
300 ml (1/2 pint) bechamel sauce
100 g (4 oz) Gruyère cheese, grated
nutmeg

Pre-heat the oven to 400°F (200°C) Gas Mark 6 and butter a gratin dish.

Steam the chunks of squash until they are just tender, then put them into the gratin dish. Pour the sauce over them and move them around a little with a fork to ensure they are all coated with the sauce. Sprinkle a generous grating of nutmeg on top, then the grated cheese and bake for 15 - 20 minutes, until the cheese has melted and is nicely brown.

Optional variations

• replace the Gruyère with thinly sliced rounds from a log of goats cheese.

• put a layer of cooked rice on the bottom of the dish.

• add a small tin of sweetcorn to the squash chunks.

Squash and tomato gratin

This is a particularly tasty gratin, and one of my favourites. In late summer, when I have plenty of home-grown tomatoes and basil, I put a layer of thick tomato slices on top, drizzle on some extra oil and add a sprinkle of torn basil leaves before baking it, to make a sort of 'roast vegetable' topping.

1 large onion, sliced
2 cloves garlic, crushed
2 tablespoons olive oil
400 g (12 oz) chopped plum tomatoes
1 teaspoon dried thyme
1 teaspoon dried oregano
salt
pepper
500 g (1 lb) thickly sliced squash flesh

Pre-heat the oven to 400°F (200°C) Gas Mark 6 and butter a gratin dish.

Fry the onion and garlic in the oil until they are tender, then add the chopped tomatoes, herbs and seasoning and cook, stirring, for 10 - 15 minutes.

Meanwhile, steam the squash slices until they are barely tender. Put them in the gratin dish and pour the sauce over them, and move them around a little with a fork to ensure they are all coated with the sauce.

Bake for 20 minutes.

Barbecued squash

Anything that can be cooked in the oven wrapped in foil can also be cooked on a barbecue (or, if you're really keen, on the exhaust manifold of your car). So try any of the recipes on page 83, omitting the baking dish and using a large piece of foil instead. To ensure all-round cooking, it is best to start cooking the squash with its cut side down, then opening the foil and adding the dressings before putting it back, cut side up, to finish cooking.

Alternatively, prepare the squash in the usual way by deseeding and peeling, then cut it into small chunks. Put these in the middle of a large piece of foil, add some thick slices of onion or leek and a generous dollop of butter, season well and seal the parcel before putting it on the barbecue to cook for 35 - 40 minutes.

Or cut thick slices from the seedless end of a Butternut squash, lay them on the barbecue grill and brush them with melted butter. Leave them for 15 minutes, turn them over and brush with more butter and some runny honey. Sprinkle on some sea salt and black pepper and let them cook another 10 minutes.

Ginger pork stew in squash shells

This is a very rich stew, so choose one of the blander tasting squash, such as Acorn. For family meals, use 2 large squash and cut them in half lengthways. For a prettier presentation, use 4 smaller squash and cut off the pointed end, so that the cut end shows the scalloped shape of the ribs.

---

4 tablespoons olive oil
500 g (1 lb) pork fillet or shoulder, in bite-sized chunks
2 medium onions, sliced
about 3cm (1") fresh ginger root
60 ml (2 fl oz) dry sherry
60 ml (2 fl oz) rich soy sauce
2 or 4 squash prepared for stuffing

Preheat the oven to 375°F (190°C) Gas Mark 5.

In a saucepan, heat the oil and seal the meat in it. When the meat is brown, add the onions and continue frying until they are translucent.

Peel and finely chop the ginger root and add it to the pan with the sherry and soy sauce. Bring the mixture to the boil and then simmer, covered, until the pork is tender - about an hour.

Place the prepared squash in a baking pan and fill them with the stew. Pour about 3cm (1") of boiling water into the pan and bake for 30 - 40 minutes, until the squash are tender.

Chicken and tomato stuffed Acorn squash

For this recipe, use one small squash per person, open them by cutting off the pointed end about a third of the way down. Save the tops for purée. You may also need to trim the bases a little so that they stand upright. This is a fairly rich stuffing, so all it needs to accompany it is some savoury rice or a crisp salad.

4 Acorn squash
2 tablespoons olive oil
2 medium onions, chopped
2 cloves garlic, crushed
4 chorizo sausages, precooked
400 g tin chopped tomatoes
300 ml (¹/₂ pint) double cream
zest of 1 lemon

Preheat the oven to 375°F (190°C) Gas Mark 5.

Prepare the squash for stuffing and place them in a roasting pan.

Fry the onions and garlic in the oil until they are translucent. Slice the sausages and add them to the pan with the tomatoes and cook until the mixture has thickened. Take the pan off the heat and stir in the cream.

Spoon the mixture into the squash, pour about 3cm (1") of boiling water into the pan and bake for 30 minutes.

Squash matafaim

'Matafaim' means 'kill hunger', the name given to a French peasant dish made at harvest time, to serve to hungry workers when they come in from the fields. The original is made with potato, but since I can't resist trying a squash version of potato dishes, I had to try this one. It needs one of the dense fleshed squashes, such as Buttercup, just as the potato version needs a floury fleshed variety. If you're really starved, you could grill some bacon to go with it.

750 g (1 ¹/₂ lbs) prepared squash flesh
2 eggs
2 cloves garlic, crushed
2 tablespoons chopped herbs (optional)
salt
pepper
nutmeg
oil for frying

Grate the squash flesh. Beat the other ingredients together and mix into the squash.

Pour a little oil into a large, preferably heavy, frying pan, and heat it for a couple of minutes before pouring in the squash mixture. (Heating the pan first will prevent the cake sticking.) Turn down the heat and cook for 10 minutes.

Turn the cake by sliding it out onto a large plate, then inverting the pan over the plate and turning both over together. Cook for another 10 minutes.

Optional variation

● add 3cm (1") fresh ginger root, finely chopped, to the grated squash.

Squash fritters

Use Acorn or Butternut squash for these delicious fritters. You don't have to cook them straightaway, so once you have made up a batch of the batter, you can keep it in your fridge for up to 2 days. A quick stir and the batter will be ready to use again.

---

2 Acorn squash
1 tablespoon plain flour
1 egg
2 - 3 tablespoons crème fraîche
2 cloves garlic, crushed
salt
pepper
oil for frying

Prepare the squash flesh and grate it. Put the flour into a bowl and add the egg and crème fraîche to make a thick batter.

Stir in the garlic and grated squash, then leave the batter to stand for about 20 minutes. Add salt and pepper to the batter just before frying, as otherwise the salt will draw water from the squash and dilute the batter.

Heat a little oil in a frying pan and fry spoonfuls of the batter for 3 - 4 minutes each side.

Optional variations

• add a tablespoonful of chopped fresh herbs to the batter.

• replace the plain flour with besan (chick-pea) flour, omit the garlic and add 1 medium onion, thinly sliced to the batter.

Pumpkin and cod fritters

This is a favourite snack in Barbados, where it is cooked and sold by vendors on the streets and beaches. Out there they use salt cod, but if you can't find it here, use raw cod fillet and cook it first.

250 g (8 oz) salt cod
100 g (4 oz) self-raising flour
1 egg
120 ml (4 fl oz) milk
2 tablespoons melted butter
250 g (8 oz) pumpkin flesh, grated
2 medium onions, chopped
1 green chilli pepper, deseeded and chopped

Soak the salt cod for at least 8 hours, changing the water several times. Then put it in a large saucepan and cover it with boiling water. Leave it to steep for 30 minutes, drain it and shred it, removing the skin and any bones.

With the flour, egg, milk and melted butter, make a batter. Mix the grated pumpkin, onion and chilli pepper into the batter, then stir in the flaked fish.

In a deep-fat fryer, drop teaspoonfuls of the mixture into the fat and fry until golden-brown - about 5 minutes. Drain well and serve hot.

Sweet and sour squash

This is a variation on a classic Sicilian pumpkin dish - 'Zucca all'agro dolce'. I think using squash rather than pumpkin gives a tastier result, but of course you could use pumpkin if you wish. It does need fresh mint, so unless you are prepared to buy a bunch of mint, it's a dish for late summer or late winter, when the squash are still usable and the mint has just started to grow. I always mean to pot up some mint at the end of summer to keep it going on my kitchen window-sill, but somehow I never get around to it.

500 g (1 lb) prepared winter squash, thinly sliced
3 tablespoons olive oil
2 cloves garlic, crushed
2 tablespoons caster sugar
4 tablespoons white wine vinegar
2 tablespoons chopped mint leaves
salt
pepper

Fry the squash in the oil until it is tender. Drain off as much of the oil as you can, then add the other ingredients to the pan. Cook until the sauce has thickened - about 10 minutes, turning the pumpkin to ensure it is well coated.

You can serve it straightaway, but it is better to let it cool and stand for several hours to allow the flavour of the sauce to completely permeate the squash, then reheat it before serving.

Squash and bacon suet rib-stickers

Suet roly-poly, with bacon and onion as a filling, was one of the most popular meals in the canteen of the office where I once used to work. My version uses leeks instead of onions, and includes squash to add flavour and a beautiful gold colour to the suet pastry. Vegetarian cooks can replace the bacon with mushroom, as I often do when I don't feel like eating meat.

And to go with it, onion gravy and celeriac and potato mash - real rib-sticking food for cold winter days.

Alternatively, omit the filling and use this dough to make dumplings to accompany any stew.

Incidentally, although most recipes use twice as much flour as suet, I found some years ago that the end result is lighter if you make that 'twice flour to suet' by volume rather than weight, which works out to three times as much flour by the weight method.

---

50 g (2 oz) butter
250 g (8 oz) streaky bacon, cut into thin strips
2 leeks, halved and sliced
2 - 3 sage leaves, snipped
pepper
300 g (12 oz) self-raising flour
100 g (4 oz) suet
pinch salt
300 g (12 oz) squash purée

Melt the butter and fry the bacon and leeks until they are done to your taste. Drain as much fat off them as you can, then add the sage and pepper.

Mix the flour, suet, salt and squash purée to a soft dough. You may need a little water, or possibly less purée, depending on how wet the purée is. Divide the dough into 4 pieces, rolling each out into a rectangle about 15 by 20 cm (6 by 9").

Divide the filling between the rectangles, spreading it out but leaving a border of about 3cm (1"). Moisten this border and roll up the dough lengthways. Wrap each roll in kitchen foil and leave it to rest for 30 minutes.

Steam the rolls, in the foil, for 45 - 50 minutes and serve hot.

Squash soufflé

Like everyone else who is frightened of making soufflés, I was agreeably surprised at how easy it was when I did finally pluck up courage to try. After all, it's only a matter of making a white sauce, adding an enhancing ingredient to it, and whipping up some egg whites to give it lift - easy peasy! This one has cheese and chives to round out the flavour of squash, and some cinnamon which gives it an unexpected zip.

Use a dry-fleshed squash, such as Buttercup, Crown Prince, or Hubbard.

---

25 g (1 oz) butter
5 tablespoons plain flour
450 ml (³/₄ pint) milk
1 egg yolk
200 g (8 oz) squash purée
1 teaspoon ground cinnamon
pinch salt
3 tablespoons snipped chives
125 g (5 oz) Gruyère cheese, grated
4 egg whites

Preheat the oven to 400°F (200°C) Gas Mark 6. Butter a 20 cm (8") soufflé dish.

Make a white sauce with the butter, flour and milk (see page 165). Beat into this the egg yolk, squash purée, cinnamon, and salt. Stir in the chives and four-fifths of the cheese.

Whisk the egg whites to stiff peaks, then fold in gently to the sauce mixture. Pour the mixture into the prepared dish and run a knife round the edge of the mixture to stick it to the dish. (This 'sealing' process prevents the soufflé rising unevenly and falling over.)

Sprinkle the rest of the cheese on top and bake for 30 minutes. Serve immediately.

Sweet Dumpling quiche

You can use any type of squash for this quiche, but Delicata or Sweet Dumpling provide the best flavour. Once it's cooked, it will last for a couple of days in the fridge - if the gannets in your household can be kept away from it.

It is good hot, as a lunch or supper dish, and equally good cold, for hot days or to take on a picnic.

---

enough short-crust pastry to line a 23cm (9") flan dish
2 small onions, chopped
25 g (1oz) butter
2 eggs, beaten
250 g (8 oz) squash purée
120 ml (4 fl oz) milk
90 ml (3 fl oz) single cream, or thick yoghurt
50 g (2 oz) Gruyère cheese, grated
salt
pepper
nutmeg

Preheat the oven to 375°F (190°C) Gas Mark 5. Line the flan dish with the pastry, and prick the bottom to prevent it rising during cooking.

Fry the onions in the butter until they are translucent, then drain them. Stir them into the beaten eggs with the squash purée, milk, cream and cheese. Season the mixture and pour it into the prepared base. Sprinkle with grated nutmeg and bake for 45 - 50 minutes.

Gingered scrambled eggs with squash

You can either make this as scrambled eggs, or lower the heat and cook it as a tortilla. Either way, it makes a tasty change from the plain version of scrambled eggs which we often have for a late breakfast at the weekend. You might want to modify the amount of garlic if you are planning to go out straightaway.

---

100 g (4 oz) prepared squash
50 g (2 oz) butter
1 clove garlic, finely chopped
3cm (1") ginger root, finely chopped
4 eggs, beaten
salt
white pepper

Cut the squash into match-stick sized batons. Melt the butter and fry the squash with the garlic and ginger until the squash is tender.

Meanwhile beat the eggs and season them to your taste. When the squash is ready, pour the eggs into the pan and scramble until they are done as you like them. Serve immediately.

Optional variations

- to make a tortilla, proceed as above, but after you have poured the eggs into the pan, turn down the heat a little and let it cook for 6 - 8 minutes, until the underside is done. Slide the tortilla out onto a plate, then turn it upside down back into the pan to cook the other side for 3 - 4 minutes.
- omit the butter and use 2 - 3 tablespoons of sesame oil.

Squash and pork sausages

I gave up eating sausages for many years, because every time I picked up a packet in the supermarket I was repelled by the long list of artificial ingredients and preservatives. Even worse were those sausages where the meat content was that 'reclaimed' mush mixed with rusk and stuffed into an artificial skin.

Then a real sausage shop opened up near to us, where the sausages are made with fresh ingredients only - and done where you can watch them while you stand at the counter. This inspired me to try making my own sausages, and this is the version that includes squash.

---

250 g (8 oz) squash flesh
500 g (1 lb) lean belly or shoulder of pork
100 g (4 oz) hard fat from the back
2 - 3 cloves garlic
1 tablespoon chopped parsley
1 tablespoon chopped sage
2 tablespoons chopped chives
1 thick slice bread, crumbed
1 teaspoon ground mace
salt
pepper
length sausage skin (see variation below if you can't
get them)

Cut the meat, fat and squash into small chunks and whizz them in your food processor until they are the texture of coarse breadcrumbs. Mix in all the other ingredients and with the aid of a large funnel, stuff it into the sausage skins. Tie a knot in one end of the skin before you start, then twist the stuffed skin into separate sausages.

Fry, grill or roast the sausages in your usual way.

Skinless variation

After mixing the ingredients together, form portions into sausage shapes and wrap these in cooking foil. Tie the ends of these with kitchen string, and drop them into simmering water for 10 minutes. Alternatively, steam them for 10 - 15 minutes. Drain them in a colander and let them cool before unwrapping them, then fry, grill or roast as above.

• Sausage skins are available by mail order from the Natural Casing Co. Ltd,
  PO Box 133, Farnham, Surrey, GU10 5HT. Tel 01252 850454

Squash and onion bhajees

If you've never shopped in an Indian grocers, you have a revelation due to you. The first time I went into one, I was entranced to discover that there are 'just add water' mixes for all the delicious things that are so time-consuming to make - idlis, dhokla, naan bread and so on. One of these mixes is for onion bhajees - just add water and onions. It works well enough if you're in a hurry, but just as a packet cheesecake mix isn't as good as home-made cheesecake, so are bhajees better if you start from scratch - and since all you have to do is mix up a batter, it's just as quick.

And equally, there is no rule that says your bhajees have to be little balls fried in deep-fat. I make them as flat cakes in an ordinary frying pan, and they taste just as good.

---

100 g (4 oz) besan (chick-pea) flour
1/2 teaspoon salt
2 teaspoons ground turmeric
2 teaspoons ground cumin
1/4 teaspoon chilli powder
75 g (3 oz) grated squash
1 medium onion, finely chopped

Sift the flour, salt and spices together, then add water, a little at a time, to make a medium thick batter. Stir the squash and onion into this.

Either drop dessertspoons of the mixture into a deep-fat fryer and fry until they are deep golden brown, or fry in vegetable oil in an ordinary frying pan as flat cakes, turning them when the first side is done. Drain well before serving.

Baked Butternut squash with sage, cream and Gruyère dressing (p84)

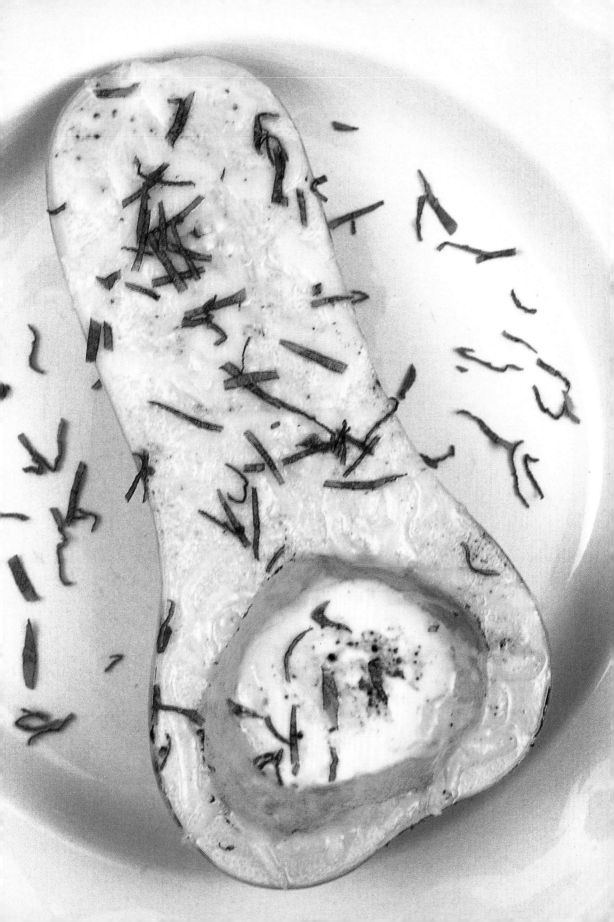

Squash Korma

Korma is the mildest of all the curries, ideal for those who do not like too much chilli.
The sauce is made with ground rather than whole spices, and includes ground nuts,
either almonds, as here, or sometimes coconut. For special occasions you could use
cream, but normally I use a thick yoghurt. Either eat it with plain boiled rice, or use it as
an additional dish to accompany a meat curry.

---

3 tablespoons vegetable oil or ghee
1 teaspoon ground coriander
1 teaspoon ground cumin
1 teaspoon ground turmeric
1/2 teaspoon ground cinnamon
1 medium onion, coarsely chopped
500 g (1 lb) prepared squash, cut in large chunks
300 ml (1/2 pint) thick yoghurt
1 teaspoon plain flour
1 tablespoon ground almonds
salt
1 tablespoon chopped coriander leaves

Heat the oil and fry the spices, stirring, for a couple of minutes. Add the onion and fry
for a couple of minutes, then the squash. You may need to add a little water to prevent it
sticking.

Lower the heat and stir in the yoghurt, a spoonful at a time. If it threatens to curdle, stir
in a little flour. Finally stir in the ground almonds, taste and season, then simmer gently
until the squash is tender - about 15 minutes.

Serve with the chopped coriander leaves sprinkled on top.

Squash roulade (p58) with Crispy courgettes Neapolitan style (p139)

Squash with coconut and paneer

Paneer is a simple cheese made by Indian cooks, which then serves as the protein content in vegetarian recipes. One of the classic recipes using it is 'matar paneer', with peas, and I have had versions of that which included coconut, so given that I had already discovered the happy marriage between squash and coconut, it was inevitable that I would try adding paneer to the equation. It worked very well, making a creamy mild dish, which you can serve with rice, or as one of several dishes when you want to cook an Indian meal.

Unless you can find a friendly Indian grocer who stocks paneer, you'll have to make your own, so I've given you the recipe for that as well. Allow 24 hours for making the paneer.

Paneer

1 litre (2 pints) milk
juice of 1 lemon, strained

In a saucepan, heat the milk until it is just at boiling point, then stir in the lemon juice and turn the heat down. Cook the mixture until it is well curdled - a couple of minutes, then turn off the heat. Pour the curdled milk into a jelly bag or a double layer of muslin, and hang it up until it stops dripping. Then turn it onto a plate or flat dish and put a weight on top to consolidate it. Put it in the fridge and leave it for about 12 hours, or until it is solid enough to cut into squares.

2 tablespoons vegetable oil or ghee
1 medium onion, chopped
2 teaspoons ground coriander
2 teaspoons turmeric
1/4 teaspoon chilli powder
3cm (1") ginger root, finely chopped
1/2 teaspoon salt
250 g (8 oz) prepared squash, in chunks
4 tablespoons water
100 g (4 oz) block of coconut cream, chopped
**   or coarsely grated paneer, as above**
3 - 4 teaspoons garam masala

Heat 1 tablespoon of the oil in a large saucepan and fry the onion until it is translucent. Stir in the spices, ginger and salt and cook for a couple of minutes, stirring. Add the squash and fry it for a couple of minutes.

Stir in the water and coconut cream, then cook gently for 10 - 15 minutes, until the squash is tender. Meanwhile, fry the paneer in the rest of the oil until it is light brown and add it to the squash mixture. Finally stir in the garam masala and cook for a further 5 minutes before serving.

Pumpkin pilau

This is a baked pilau made with cooked rice, which we like so much that I always cook too much rice so that there is enough left to do this the next day. In its simplest form, all you add to it is some fried onions, some raisins, and some flaked almonds on top, but here you add some little cubes of pumpkin or squash. It's a meal on its own, but if you like something moister, just add a curry sauce.

---

250 g (8 oz) long grain rice - ideally basmati
salt
2 medium onions, thinly sliced
1 tablespoon vegetable oil
50 g (2 oz) raisins
250 g (8 oz) prepared pumpkin or squash, in small cubes
4 tablespoons stock
50 g (2 oz) flaked almonds

Cook the rice by your usual method. Pour boiling water over the raisins and leave them to plump up. Fry the onions in the oil until they are starting to go brown.

Preheat the oven to 375°F (190°C) Gas Mark 5.

Mix the fried onions and raisins into the cooked rice and put it into a casserole. In a saucepan, pour the stock over the pumpkin cubes and bring it to the boil before adding it to the casserole. Stir well so that the pumpkin is mixed right through the rice. Put the lid on and bake for 50 minutes covered, then remove the lid and sprinkle the flaked almonds over the top before baking for a further 15 - 20 minutes.

Serve from the casserole so that diners can see the toasted almonds.

Tiny pumpkins stuffed with Stilton cheese

There are several varieties of tiny pumpkins, with names such as Baby Boo, Munchkin, or Jack Be Little, any of which are suitable for this recipe. Or you could use Acorn or Sweet Dumpling squash. Cut the tops off carefully and replace them before you bake the pumpkins, so that each diner can take hold of the stalk and lift their own lid.

---

4 tiny pumpkins
2 tablespoons olive oil
4 spring onions, chopped
2 cloves garlic, crushed
100 g (4 oz) streaky bacon, cut small
2 large tomatoes
100 g (4 oz) Stilton cheese
4 tablespoons crème fraîche

Preheat the oven to 450°F (230°C) Gas Mark 8.

Prepare the pumpkins for stuffing.

Heat the oil and fry the onions, garlic and bacon for 5 minutes. Skin the tomatoes and squeeze the pips out, then chop flesh and add to the frying pan. Cook another 5 minutes, then take the pan from the heat.

Crumble the cheese and mix it into the fried mixture, then use this to fill the pumpkins. Put a spoonful of crème fraîche on top of each, then replace the 'lids' before putting the pumpkins in a baking pan. Pour in boiling water to about 3cm (1") deep, then bake for 30 minutes.

Loosen the tops with a knife before serving.

Squash, potato and apple mash

Squash, mashed on its own with butter and pepper, is a delicious change from ordinary mashed potato. If you like dry mash, go for one of the really dry-fleshed squashes, such as Buttercup, Crown Prince or Hubbard, otherwise choose any of the golden-fleshed varieties.

But for a real treat, try this mixture of squash, potato and apple mashed together. It makes an excellent accompaniment for rich meats such as pork, ham or sausages. Make more than you need for one meal, then tip the spare into a flat baking dish, and drag a fork over the top to rough it up. The next day, bake it in a medium oven for about 20 minutes to heat through and crisp up the top.

---

1 kilo (2 lbs) prepared squash
1 kilo (2 lbs) peeled potatoes
    (choose a floury variety, such as Cara, Desiree, or Wilja)
500 g (1 lb) cooking apples, ideally Bramley
salt
white pepper
butter

Cut the squash, potatoes and apples into equal sized chunks and steam them, either separately or together, until they are tender. Tip them into a large bowl, add salt and pepper and as much butter as you dare, and mash to your favourite consistency.

Turn the mash into a serving dish and take it to the table.

Optional variations

- add some grated nutmeg before mashing, or sprinkle it over the top of the dishful before serving.

Tip

- over-mashing potato tends to make it gluey, so once it is as you like it, stop mashing.

Squash and pumpkin purées

There are a number of these purées, designed to be served as a side dish with meat, poultry or fish. In each case, you can serve them either as they come from the puréeing process, or pop them into the oven to reheat and crisp up the top. For fancy occasions, instead of peeling the squash before cooking, start by halving it raw, removing the seeds, then steaming or baking it until it is tender. Then scoop out the flesh, follow the recipe and finally return the finished purée to the empty shells to bake.

In all cases, bake at 400°F (200°C) Gas Mark 6 for 15 minutes if hot, 25 minutes if cold.

Creamed pumpkin

1 medium onion, chopped
2 tablespoons olive oil
500 g (1 lb) pumpkin purée
1 teaspoon ground ginger
1/2 teaspoon ground allspice
1/4 teaspoon grated nutmeg
salt
crisp fried bacon bits (optional)

Fry the onion in the oil until tender, then beat in the pumpkin and spices. Serve with the bacon sprinkled on top.

African pumpkin 'ambrosia'

450 ml (3/4 pint) salted water
150 g (6 oz) cornmeal or polenta
250 g (8 oz) mashed pumpkin
1/2 teaspoon granulated sugar
2 tablespoons smooth peanut butter

Bring the salted water to the boil and pour in the cornmeal, then cook for 20 minutes, stirring constantly until it becomes porridge-like. Beat in the pumpkin, then add the other ingredients and beat well. If it seems too thick, add a little more boiling water.

Cranberry squash purée

2 Acorn squash, puréed
100 g (4 oz) butter
2 tablespoons granulated sugar
2 tablespoons white wine
pinch ground allspice
1 tablespoon cranberry jelly or 50 g (2 oz)
    fresh cranberries, chopped
salt

Put all the ingredients in a large saucepan over a gentle heat and cook for 10 minutes, stirring well. Taste and add salt to your taste, then cook another 2 minutes before serving.

Squash purée sweetened with maple syrup

500 g (1 lb) dense-fleshed squash, such as Buttercup or
    Crown Prince, puréed
75 g (3 oz) butter
1 teaspoon ground ginger
3 tablespoons maple syrup
1 tablespoon chopped parsley

Beat the butter, ginger and maple syrup into the squash purée, then serve garnished with the parsley.

Savoury Butternut squash purée

1 spring onion, chopped
2 cloves garlic, crushed
1 fresh green chilli, deseeded and chopped finely
1 tablespoon olive oil
500 g (1 lb) Butternut squash purée
2 tablespoons chopped fresh herbs - thyme, parsley, sage,
    basil, or a mixture of all
25 g (1 oz) butter

Fry the onion, garlic and chilli in the oil until tender, then drain them on a piece of kitchen paper before stirring them into the purée with the herbs. Add little dots of butter to the top just before serving.

Pumpkin armandine

500 g (1 lb) coarsely mashed pumpkin
250 ml (8 fl oz) bechamel sauce made with half milk
and half single cream
50 g (2 oz) flaked almonds, toasted

With a fork, mix the pumpkin into the sauce and sprinkle the toasted almonds on top just before serving.

Pumpkin with potato and cheese

500 g (1 lb) potato
500 g (1 lb) prepared pumpkin
100 g (4 oz) butter
salt
white pepper
100 g (4 oz) Gruyère cheese, grated
25 g (1 oz) Parmesan cheese, grated (optional)

Chop the potato and pumpkin into equal sized chunks and cook them together. Ideally this should be by steaming, as boiling will make the pumpkin rather wet. Mash them coarsely with the butter, salt and pepper, then beat in the Gruyère. If you choose to finish this dish by baking it, sprinkle the Parmesan on top first.

Squash and pork stuffing for turkey or chicken

This is a replacement for the traditional chestnut stuffing. I find tinned chestnut purée unsatisfactory, as it tends to be bitter, and although I love whole fresh chestnuts, in any form, they are a time-consuming fiddle to peel properly. So as soon as I discovered how like chestnut some of the denser-fleshed squash are, I tried it as a substitute. It isn't quite the same, but it's tasty and a lot better than tinned chestnut purée. Use Buttercup, Crown Prince, or Hubbard squash.

---

500 g (1 lb) prepared squash flesh
750 g (1 1/2 lbs) pork sausage meat
3 thick slices of bread, crumbed
2 - 3 tablespoons chopped parsley
1 tablespoon chopped sage
2 medium onions, finely chopped
2 eggs, beaten
salt
pepper

Chop the squash into cubes about 1/2 cm (1/4") across and mix them well with all the other ingredients. Use this to stuff your bird and cook it in the usual way.

Optional variation

● add 15 - 20 pre-soaked prunes, quartered, to the stuffing mix.

Baked squash, with flavoured toppings

As a simple side dish, squash baked in its skin then scooped out by the diner, takes some beating. However, some people feel that a little more is needed, so here are some toppings for added flavour. Each recipe will dress 4 halves of squash.

In each case, halve the squash and scoop out the seeds. You may need to cut a bit off the bottom to make them sit more steadily in the pan. Then score the flesh a little to allow the flavours to permeate before adding the topping. Cover the roasting pan with foil to start cooking, then remove it for about 10 minutes at the end to allow the squash to dry out a little and brown the top. Small squash such as Acorns will need about 30 minutes to cook, larger specimens about 40 - 45 minutes. Test for doneness with a skewer, which should pass easily right through.

You can also prepare slices of larger specimens, which will take 20 - 25 minutes to cook.

Coconut cream and lime dressing

2 tablespoons coconut cream, grated from a block
2 teaspoons lime juice
1 tablespoon dessicated coconut

Mix the coconut cream and lime juice together and warm them gently until the coconut has melted. Spoon this mixture over the squash, then sprinkle the dessicated coconut on top.

Honey and hazelnut dressing

4 tablespoons runny honey
4 teaspoons chopped hazelnuts
4 small pinches ground allspice

Mix the ingredients together and spoon them over the squash before serving.

Sage, cream and Gruyère dressing

4 sage leaves, snipped finely
120 ml (4 fl oz) single cream
100 g (4 oz) Gruyère cheese, grated
2 teaspoons thyme leaves

Stir the sage into the cream. Sprinkle the cheese onto the squash, spoon the sage cream over it, then finish with a sprinkle of thyme.

Cream and pine nut dressing

8 tablespoons single cream
1 teaspoon ground coriander
2 teaspoons thyme leaves
2 tablespoons pine nuts

Spoon the cream over the squash, then sprinkle on the herbs and pine nuts.

Butter, garlic and rosemary dressing

> **100 g (4 oz) butter, melted**
> **2 cloves garlic, chopped very finely**
> **1 teaspoon rosemary, chopped very finely**
> **black pepper**

Mix all the ingredients together before spooning the dressing over the squash.

Martinique dressing

> **100 g (4 oz) butter**
> **marrow from about 10cm (4") beef bone**
> **1 teaspoon ground ginger**
> **pepper**

There are two ways to prepare this dressing. Either melt the butter and the bone marrow, mix them together and spoon them over the squash before sprinkling the ginger and pepper on top. Or slice the butter and marrow thinly, arrange the slices on the squash and sprinkle the ginger and pepper on top.

Roast squash ball trio

I'm very fond of roast vegetables, and often serve either chunked potatoes on their own, or mixed with onions, tomatoes and squash, basted with olive oil and chopped rosemary. But it's more fun, for special occasions, to serve little balls of flesh from different coloured squash. Alternatively, you could cut the squash into slices and cut shapes out with a cookie cutter.

> **2 cloves garlic, crushed**
> **1 tablespoon finely chopped, fresh rosemary**
> **4 tablespoons olive oil**
> **1 gold fleshed squash, such as Butternut**
> **2 cream fleshed squash, such as Acorn, Sweet Dumpling**
> **or Delicata**
> **1 deep orange fleshed squash, such as Buttercup,**
> **Crown Prince, Hubbard, or Kabocha**

Preheat the oven to 350°F (180°C) Gas Mark 4.

Stir the garlic and rosemary into the oil and leave it to infuse.

Cut each squash in half and remove the seeds. With a melon baller, scoop out as many balls of flesh as you can. (Save the rest to make purée.)

Put the balls into a roasting pan and pour the oil over them, then turn them with a spoon to ensure they are all covered with oil. Roast them for 25 - 30 minutes, basting them with the oil at least once.

Alternatively, roast them in the pan with meat or poultry, using the meat juices to baste them.

Pumpkin or squash chips

Yes, you can make chips with squash, but unlike potato chips, you do need to degorge the squash or the end result will be soggy. The easiest squash to use is Butternut, because the seedless end has plenty of flesh to cut into batons, but you could also use any of the larger dense fleshed squash, such as Buttercup or Crown Prince.

Prepare the squash by peeling and deseeding it, then cut it into chip shapes. Lay these in a colander and sprinkle them liberally with salt, then leave them to degorge for at least 30 minutes. Rinse them well and dry them, then shake some plain flour over them before deep frying them in the normal way. Peanut oil is best.

Squash crisps

As above, prepare the squash and cut the flesh into very thin slices. If you don't have a mandolin, a vegetable peeler is probably the best way to do it. It isn't necessary to degorge these thin slices. After frying and draining them, dredge some paprika, or garlic salt, over them.

Pumpkin seeds

The seeds of all the squashes and pumpkins are edible, but many varieties have such tough seed coats that it is too much effort for most people to get at the seeds. If you want to grow your own seeds, choose one of the 'hull-less' varieties such as Triple Treat. Otherwise, just buy your pumpkin seeds at a health food shop.

With home-grown seeds, if you want to keep them any length of time, you have to dry them out to prevent them rotting. Remove all the accompanying fibres then either lay them out on sheets of kitchen paper and leave them for several days in a warm dry place, or spread them out on a baking tray and give them 10 - 15 minutes in a very cool oven.

You can then eat them as they are, or dress them up a little to serve as nibbles with drinks.

Curried pumpkin seeds

> **1 tablespoon curry powder**
> **2 tablespoons water**
> **juice of ½ lemon**
> **250 g (8 oz) pumpkin seeds**
> **2 tablespoons salt**

Mix the curry powder with the water and lemon juice over a gentle heat, then add the pumpkin seeds and give them a stir to coat them with the liquid. Cook them for about 5 minutes, until the liquid has evaporated. Drain them well on kitchen paper, then sprinkle them with salt and leave them to cool before serving.

Caramelised pumpkin seeds

> **50 g (2 oz) saltless butter**
> **250 g (8 oz) pumpkin seeds**
> **2 tablespoons sugar**
> **juice of ½ lemon**

Melt the butter in a frying pan, then add the pumpkin seeds and cook, stirring, over a low heat, for 3 - 4 minutes. Take care that the butter doesn't burn. Turn the seeds out of the pan onto kitchen paper, toss them to remove most of the butter and wipe out the pan.

Put the seeds back in the clean pan with sugar and lemon juice and toss over a low heat until the sugar has melted. Again, watch them carefully to prevent sugar burning. Take the pan off the heat and let the seeds cool, stirring if needed to keep them separate.

Savoury squash and cheese puffs

Makes 24

These are tasty little mouthfuls, which you can make in bun cases, or in eclair or madeleine moulds. With grated raw squash in them, they stay moist inside while the outside is crisp. Use Acorn squash, or in summer, courgette.

---

2 large eggs, beaten
2 tablespoons crème fraîche or thick yoghurt
2 tablespoons milk
2 teaspoons made mustard
2 teaspoons chopped marjoram
1 tablespoon chopped chives
3 cloves garlic, finely chopped
1/2 teaspoon cayenne pepper
1/4 teaspoon salt
150 g (6 oz) grated raw squash
50 g (2 oz) Cheddar cheese, finely grated

Preheat the oven to 425°F (220°C) Gas Mark 7 and grease baking tins - bun-mould, eclair or madeleine shaped.

Beat all the ingredients together before putting about a dessertspoonful in each compartment of your baking tin. Bake for 15 - 20 minutes, until a skewer comes out clean. Turn out onto a wire rack to cool.

Breads

Squash focaccia

Focaccia is a very light Italian bread. For the authentic soft crumb, you should use pasta flour (grade 00), but if you can't get this, ordinary 'strong' bread flour works almost as well, although the crumb will be denser. Traditionally, focaccia is topped with herbs, sliced onion, and sometimes tomato. I wondered how it would work with squash purée added to the dough, and slices of squash on top, and was delighted to find that it works very well.

You need a fairly dry fleshed squash such as Buttercup or Crown Prince for this recipe, as your purée should be fairly dry.

2¹/₂ teaspoons dried active or 'easy blend' yeast
200 ml (6 fl oz) warm water
750 g (1¹/₂ lbs) flour
1 teaspoon fine salt
500 g (1 lb) dryish squash purée
2 tablespoons olive oil
1 clove garlic, crushed
1 teaspoon chopped rosemary or thyme
100 g (4 oz) prepared squash flesh in one piece
coarse salt
black pepper

Put the warm water into a small bowl, sprinkle the yeast over it and leave it to foam for about 10 minutes.

Rub the squash purée into all but 50 g (2 oz) of the flour until it resembles fine bread-crumbs. This can be done in a food processor. Add the yeast and water and work the mixture to a dough. Spread a little of the remaining flour on the work surface, turn the dough out onto this and knead it for 8 - 10 minutes, sprinkling it with the rest of the flour as needed.

Put the dough into a large plastic bag and stand it in a warm place to rise until it is doubled in size - about 90 minutes. Meanwhile, mix the garlic and rosemary into the olive oil and leave it to stand.

Grease a baking tray or dish - a Swiss roll tin is about the right size. Turn the dough into this tin and spread it out into the corners, using your knuckles to move it. Cover the tin with a clean tea-towel, and return it to the warm place to rise again until it is doubled in size - about 45 minutes. Turn the oven on to preheat to 400°F (200°C) Gas Mark 6.

Slice the squash flesh into paper-thin slices, and arrange these, overlapping, on top of the dough. Brush the olive oil mixture on top of the slices, and finally sprinkle the coarse salt and the pepper over them.

Bake it in the bottom of the oven for 45 - 50 minutes. Let it cool in the pan for 20 minutes before turning it out.

Squash bread

This gives a beautiful golden loaf, which keeps well, and can be eaten with savoury or sweet toppings. The best squash to use is one of the dry-fleshed varieties such as Buttercup, Crown Prince or Hubbard. You can use others, but if you do, I suggest you use less squash, or be prepared to add more flour. Experience will allow you to adjust as necessary, once you've seen the texture you need.

For parties, or just when you want to amuse the family, make a loaf that looks like a pumpkin. Pull off a little piece of dough for the 'stem', form the rest into a round and flatten it slightly. Cut 8 - 9 vertical slashes round the sides to make the segmented shape and add the 'stem' at the top.

---

3 level teaspoons dried active or 'easy blend' yeast
4 tablespoons hand-hot water
500 g (1 lb) squash purée
550 g (18 oz) strong white bread flour
1 teaspoon salt
1 tablespoon olive oil

In a small bowl, sprinkle the yeast over the warm water and leave it to froth for about 10 minutes.

Rub the squash purée into all but 50 g (2 oz) of the flour until it resembles fine bread-crumbs. This can be done in a food processor. Add the yeast, salt and oil, and work the mixture into a ball of dough.

Sprinkle a little of the remaining flour on to your work-surface, adding more as needed, and knead the dough for 10 minutes. Sprinkle a little more flour over the dough, then put it into a large plastic bag and stand it in a warm place to rise until it is doubled in size - about 90 minutes.

Sprinkle some flour into a loaf tin, or onto a flat baking sheet. Knead the dough again briefly and form it into a loaf shape, fitting this into the tin or standing it on the baking tray, and return it to the warm place, covered with a clean tea-towel, to rise again for about 60 minutes.

Meanwhile, preheat the oven to 375°F (190°C) Gas Mark 5.

Bake the loaf in the bottom of the oven for 55 - 60 minutes. Turn it out of the tin straight away, as otherwise it can get soggy from condensation.

Squash bread (p90), Squash dinner rolls (p92),
Pumpkins and orange jam (p100) and Baby Pattypans in oil (p106)

Optional variations

- for a spicy tea-loaf version add 1 teaspoon each of ground cinnamon and ginger and 1/2 teaspoon of nutmeg to the dry ingredients, then at the second knead, flatten the dough and sprinkle 50 g (2 oz) sultanas on before kneading them in well.
- for a cheese and chives version, add 50 - 75 g (2 - 3 oz) grated Cheddar cheese and 2 tablespoons snipped fresh chives to the dry ingredients.
- for a curry version, add 1 tablespoon curry powder, 1/2 teaspoon chilli powder, and 2 tablespoons cumin seeds to the dry ingredients.

Squash bread - breadmaker version

Like many busy cooks, I have a bread-making machine. I love it, not only because it allows me to make fancier bread than I can buy at a reasonable price, but also because I can just dump in all the ingredients and leave the machine to do the whole job for me. Once you've got used to the texture needed for squash bread, you can do that too, but I suggest that the first time you do it the way I describe below.

4 tablespoons hand-hot water
2 level teaspoons dried active or 'easy blend' yeast
350 g (13 oz) squash purée
350 g (13 oz) strong white bread flour
1 teaspoon salt
1 tablespoon olive oil

Put the water into the bucket and sprinkle the yeast over it, then leave it for 10 minutes to froth.

Mix the squash purée into the flour until it resembles fine breadcrumbs. This can be done in a food processor. When the yeast is ready, put the flour into the bucket, add the salt and oil, put the bucket into the machine and set it for its standard (not quick) cycle.

Keeping your face and hands well away from the machine, start it with the lid open and watch the kneading process. If the mixture looks too dry, add a little more water, a tablespoon at a time. Once you are happy that all is going well, shut the lid and leave the machine to get on with it.

Spicy tea-loaf variation

- add 1 teaspoon each of ground cinnamon and ginger and 1/2 teaspoon of grated nutmeg to the dry ingredients. Set the machine for its 'special bread' programme, then when it beeps at you to tell you it's ready, open the lid and sprinkle 50 g (2 oz) sultanas over the dough as it kneads.

Squash pancakes (p110)

Squash dinner rolls

Makes 12 rolls

These rolls are a little lighter in texture and colour than the squash bread, but otherwise they are no more difficult to make than the bread. You can make them in the usual round roll shape, or ring the changes by producing knots or small plaits.

---

3 level teaspoons dried active or 'easy blend' yeast
2 tablespoons granulated sugar
4 tablespoons hand-hot water
250 g (8 oz) squash purée
550 g (18 oz) strong white bread flour
1 teaspoon salt
1 tablespoon olive oil
1 tablespoon melted butter or milk
1 tablespoon poppy or sesame seeds (optional)

In a small bowl, sprinkle the yeast and sugar over the warm water and leave it to froth for about 10 minutes.

Mix the squash purée into all but 50 g (2 oz) of the flour until it resembles fine bread-crumbs. This can be done in a food processor. Add the yeast liquid, salt and oil, and work the mixture into a ball of dough.

Sprinkle a little of the remaining flour on to your work-surface, adding more as needed, and knead the dough for 10 minutes. Sprinkle a little more flour over the dough, then put it into a large plastic bag and stand it in a warm place to rise until it is doubled in size - about 90 minutes.

Sprinkle some flour onto a flat baking sheet. Knead the dough again briefly and divide it into 12 pieces. For plain round rolls, just form each piece into a ball. For knots, roll each piece into a strip and tie a knot in it. For plaits, instead of dividing the dough into small pieces, divide it into 3 and roll each into a strip before plaiting them together, then cut the plait into roll lengths, pinching the ends together.

Arrange the rolls on the baking tray, and return it to the warm place, covered with a clean tea-towel, to rise again for about 60 minutes.

Meanwhile, preheat the oven to 375°F (190°C) Gas Mark 5.

Paint a little melted butter or milk over the top of each roll, sprinkle on the poppy or sesame seeds. Bake the rolls in the bottom of the oven for 20 minutes.

Cornbread with squash and pepper

Cornbreads are made with cornmeal or polenta, which is just another name for the same thing. They are served from the cooking pan, and this gives them their alternate name of spoonbreads. Because cornmeal contains no gluten, they don't rise, but that doesn't make them any less tasty. Serve this one with grilled or roast meat, stews, or just on its own as an interesting lunch dish.

---

100 g (4 oz) sweetcorn
100 g (4 oz) prepared squash, ideally Hubbard
1/2 red pepper
1 medium onion
50 g (2 oz) cornmeal or polenta
1 teaspoon baking powder
1 teaspoon paprika
1/2 teaspoon chilli powder
1 teaspoon salt
1 teaspoon granulated sugar
300 ml (1/2 pint) milk
50 g (2 oz) butter
2 eggs, beaten

Preheat the oven to 400°F (200°C) Gas Mark 6 and grease a small baking pan - about 20cm (8") square.

Chop the squash, onion and pepper to pieces about the same size as the sweetcorn kernels. Steam all the vegetables briefly, or cook them for 3 - 4 minutes in a microwave oven. Drain them.

Sift the dry ingredients together. Put the milk and butter in a saucepan and bring them to just short of boiling point. Take the pan off the heat and gradually add the cornmeal mixture, stirring to avoid lumps. Then stir in the vegetables and egg, mixing well.

Pour this mixture into the greased pan. You may think it looks far too wet, but don't worry about this, as the cornmeal will expand during cooking.

Bake for 25 - 30 minutes, until the top is golden brown and a skewer comes out clean.

Serve warm, straight from the pan.

Pumpkin damper

'Damper' is the name given by Boy Scouts to a simple flour and water paste 'bread' which they wrap round a stick and hold close to the camp-fire. When you've finished shuddering at that thought, read on, and you'll find that this isn't a variation on that recipe. In this case, the damper is a quick loaf made with self-raising flour, baked very quickly in the oven. It's not a bread for keeping, but if you need some bread in a hurry when the shops are shut, this one is easy to make and tastes very good.

---

550 g (18 oz) self-raising flour
$1/2$ teaspoon salt
50 g (2 oz) butter
350 g (12 oz) pumpkin purée
90 ml (3 fl oz) water

Preheat the oven to 450°F (230°C) Gas Mark 8.

Sift 500 g (1 lb) of the flour and salt into a mixing bowl and rub in the butter. Add the pumpkin purée and enough of the water to make a sticky dough.

Sprinkle some of the remaining flour onto your work surface, turn the dough out onto it and knead it until it is smooth. Form it into a rough ball-shape and put this on a well-floured baking tray. Cut a shallow cross in the top and sift a little flour over it.

Bake it for 10 minutes, then turn the heat down to 375°F (190°C) Gas Mark 5 for another 20 - 30 minutes. To test whether it is done, lift it off the tray and knock the bottom with your knuckles. It should sound hollow.

Eat it hot or cold, ideally within 4 hours of making.

Pumpkin Johnnycake

Johnnycakes are traditional easy-to-make American breads, made with corn (maize) meal and molasses. Quick to whip up and quick to bake, they are another answer to the "Oh no, I haven't got any bread and the shops are shut" problem.

---

350 g (12 oz) pumpkin purée
250 g (8 oz) black molasses (or golden syrup)
125 g (5 oz) plain flour
100 g (4 oz) cornmeal (or polenta)
250 ml (8 fl oz) sour milk
pinch salt
1 egg, beaten

Preheat the oven to 350°F (180°C) Gas Mark 4 and grease a baking pan - about 20cm (8") square.

Mix all the ingredients together to a smooth batter. Pour it into the baking pan and bake for 30 minutes. Cool and serve in squares straight from the pan.

Tip

● the easiest way to weigh treacle, golden syrup or honey, is to weigh the jarful, work out what it should weigh when you've removed the desired quantity, then spoon it out until you've arrived at the second weight. If you dip the spoon into very hot water, or some vegetable oil, before you start spooning, the sticky stuff will come off quicker.

Squash 'Fluden'

Serves 10 - 12

Fluden is a traditional Jewish cake, made of thin layers of rich yeast pastry interspersed with layers of plum jam, apple, nuts and raisins, and poppyseeds. It looks wonderful, with its different coloured layers, and as soon as I encountered it, I wondered if it would work in a savoury version. Here's the results of my experiments, replacing the sweet layers with squash, onion, mushroom and spinach.

Pastry

5 tablespoons warm milk
1 tablespoon sugar
2 teaspoons dried active or 'easy blend' yeast
500 g (1 lb) plain flour
500 g (1 lb) butter
4 eggs, beaten
8 tablespoons dry white wine

Fillings

200 g (7 oz) squash purée
200 g (7 oz) onion, chopped
200 g (7 oz) butter
200 g (7 oz) chopped mushrooms
200 g (7 oz) chopped spinach

Stir the sugar and yeast into the warm milk and leave it to froth.

Sift the flour into a mixing bowl and rub in the butter. Add the eggs, wine, and yeast mix and knead to a smooth dough. Cover the bowl with a clean tea-towel and leave it to rest for an hour.

Meanwhile, assemble and prepare the fillings. Purée the squash, and in three separate pans, fry the onions in one third of the butter, fry the mushrooms in another third of the butter, and cook the spinach in the rest of the butter and whatever water remains on it after washing. If you feel these fillings are too greasy, drain them before using.

Preheat the oven to 350°F (180°C) Gas Mark 4 and grease a baking pan - I used a standard sized roasting tin.

Divide the dough into five pieces and roll each out to fit your baking pan. Put the first piece in the pan, add a layer of one of the fillings, lay another piece of dough on top and pinch the sides together. Repeat with the other fillings, ending with a layer of dough. Brush the top with beaten egg and bake the fluden for 40 minutes.

Serve it in thin slices with a crisp green salad.

Jam, chutneys, pickles, relishes, biscuits, cakes and puddings

All the winter and summer squashes make excellent jams, pickles and chutneys.

If you've never made these before, you need to know how to sterilise your jars, and when the mixture is ready for bottling.

- prepare your jam-jars by washing and drying them, then placing them upside-down in the oven. Heat the oven to 250°F (120°C) Gas Mark ½ and leave the jars for 15 minutes, then turn off the oven and leave the jars to cool slightly. They should still be warm when you fill them. Sterilize the lids by pouring boiling water over them.

- you can also sterilise jam-jars in a microwave oven. Quarter fill them with water and microwave on HIGH until the water comes to the boil. Remove the jars from the oven, pour out the water, and stand them upside-down on kitchen paper or a clean tea-cloth until you are ready to fill them.

- test for readiness in the usual way, by dropping a little on a cold china plate to see if it stays in place when you tip the plate.

- pour the mixture into the prepared jars and leave it to cool before putting on the lids. If you put a cold lid on a hot jarful of jam or chutney, condensation will form a layer of water on top of the contents.

- jams and chutneys with large chunks of flesh or zest in them should be allowed to cool before bottling, as otherwise the chunks will rise to the top.

Acorn squash 'butter'

I was making quince 'butter' with the last of the quinces and realised that the mixture I was stirring had very much the texture of Acorn squash flesh, so I experimented the next day and found that it worked perfectly. You could also use Sweet Dumpling or Delicata squash if you have them. As it is very high in sugar content, this 'butter' keeps for a long time. It's delicious on squash scones or pumpkin bread as well as on ordinary bread.

---

flesh of 1 large Acorn squash, puréed finely
150 g (6 oz) granulated sugar
25 g (1 oz) butter
juice of ½ lemon

(These quantities will give 1 jar full of 'butter')

Put all the ingredients in a large saucepan or preserving pan and cook it over a gentle heat, stirring constantly until it thickens. This should take about 15 - 20 minutes, depending on the quantity you are making. Test it for readiness in the usual way.

When it is ready, pour it into the jars and seal them.

Squash and ginger jam

Unlike many of the recipes you see for Marrow and Ginger jam, this one has a roundness of flavour introduced by the squash and apple, and an added dimension from the cinnamon. It goes well with any of the squash breads, buns or scones. Use any type of squash for this recipe.

---

1 kilo (2 lbs) prepared squash
500 g (1 lb) prepared cooking apple - ideally Bramley
150 ml ($^1/_4$ pint) water
1 kilo (2 lbs) light brown sugar
75 g (3 oz) ginger root, grated
$^1/_2$ teaspoon powdered cinnamon
25 g (1 oz) stem ginger, finely chopped

(These quantities will give 5 - 6 jars full of jam)

Chop the squash and apple into very small pieces and cook these in the water until they are soft enough to mash. Transfer the result to a preserving pan, add all the other ingredients, and cook, stirring constantly, until it thickens. This should take about 15 - 20 minutes, depending on the quantity you are making. Test for readiness in the usual way.

When it is ready, pour it into the jars and seal them.

Optional variation

• omit the ginger, add 450 g (1 lb) chopped kumquats.

Pumpkin marmalade

This isn't a true marmalade because you use sweet oranges rather than Sevilles, but it tastes just as good. It looks pretty in the jars, too, with quarters of orange complete with their peel.

---

2 kilos (4 lbs) prepared pumpkin
2 kilos (4 lbs) granulated sugar
600 ml (1 pint) water
3 large navel or other pipless oranges

(These quantities will give 5 - 6 jars full of marmalade)

Cut the pumpkin into small chunks and place them in a preserving pan with the sugar. Give it a good shake to spread the sugar all over the pumpkin. Cover the pan and leave it to stand for several hours, during which time the sugar will draw the juice out of the pumpkin.

Add the water to the pan of pumpkin and sugar, and start it cooking over a high heat while you prepare the oranges. Cut these into quarters lengthways, then into thin slices, and when the pumpkin mix is boiling, add them to the pan. Wait until the mixture is boiling again, then turn it down to a fast simmer and cook until the pumpkin and oranges are tender. This should take about 15 minutes.

Continue simmering until setting point is reached. Resist the urge to stir the mixture any more than necessary to prevent it sticking, as over-stirring will break up the orange pieces.

When the marmalade is at setting point, draw it away from the heat and let it cool for 15 minutes before putting it in the jars. If you put it in jars while it is too hot, the orange slices will rise to the top as it sets.

Pumpkin and orange jam

If, like me, you don't care for marmalade with peel in it, this jam is the answer. It has all the flavour of Seville oranges, without the dreaded peel to get in your teeth. Instead, it looks rather like apricot conserve, both in colour and texture.

It is also a useful ingredient for several of the squash puddings which follow.

---

10 small Seville oranges
900 ml (1 1/2 pints) water
750 g (1 1/2 lbs) granulated sugar
1 kilo (2 lbs) pumpkin purée

(This quantity will make 5 - 6 jars of jam)

With a zester, strip all the zest from the orange skins and put it in a preserving pan. Now cut the oranges in half and squeeze the juice out, adding that to the preserving pan. Save the pips and other residue from the top of the squeezer, and boil this for a couple of minutes in a little of the water, then strain the liquid into the preserving pan.

Add the rest of the water, the sugar, and the pumpkin purée, stirring well to incorporate all the ingredients. Bring the mixture up to the boil, then turn the heat down to a fast simmer, stirring frequently until it has thickened and reached setting point.

When it is ready, pour it into the warm jars, then let it cool a little before sealing them.

Optional variation

• Use lemons instead of Seville oranges.

Pumpkin and pineapple jam

This jam has the same texture as the pumpkin and orange jam, but instead of the hint of bitterness that comes from Seville oranges, this has the sharp sweetness of pineapples.

---

3 x 425 g tins of crushed pineapple in pineapple juice
900 ml (1 1/2 pints) water
750 g (1 1/2 lbs) granulated sugar
1 kilo (2 lbs) pumpkin purée

(This quantity will make 6 - 7 jars of jam)

Put all the ingredients in a preserving pan. Bring the mixture up to the boil, then turn the heat down to a fast simmer, stirring until it has thickened and reached setting.

When it is ready, pour it into the warm jars, then let it cool a little before sealing them.

Sweet Dumpling jam

The chestnut-like flavour of the Sweet Dumpling squash is emphasised in this jam by adding some actual chestnuts. If you don't have time to deal with fresh chestnuts, or you want to make this jam towards the end of winter when fresh chestnuts aren't available but your stock of squash needs using up, you can use dried or vacuum-packed chestnuts instead. Tinned chestnut purée is not a good substitute, as it tends to be bitter. Acorn or Delicata squash will stand in for the Sweet Dumpling.

---

500 g (1 lb) cooked chestnuts
1 kilo (2 lbs) prepared squash
6 drops vanilla essence
1 kilo (2 lbs) light brown sugar
450 ml (^{3}/4 pint) water

(These quantities will give 5 - 6 jars full of jam)

If you are using fresh chestnuts, cook and peel them and break them up into pieces. If using dried chestnuts, cover them in boiling water and leave them to soak for 12 hours. Check them over and remove any pieces of skin, then cook them in boiling water for 5 - 10 minutes. Drain and break them up into pieces.

Cut the squash into small dice, cover these with the sugar and leave to macerate for about 2 hours.

Put all the ingredients into a preserving pan and cook, stirring constantly, for about 20 minutes, removing any scum that surfaces. Draw the pan off the heat and mash the contents, bring it back to simmering and continue to cook until it reaches setting point.

When it is ready, pour it into the jars and seal them.

Pumpkin and fennel pickle

This sweet pickle has overtones of aniseed from the fennel flesh and seeds, which makes it a good accompaniment to fish dishes. It also goes well with cheese sandwiches made with pumpkin or squash bread. It needs to be kept for 2 - 3 months to allow the full flavour to develop.

---

1 kilo (2 lbs) prepared pumpkin
2 bulbs fennel
1 tablespoon fennel seed
225 g (8 oz) honey
1 tablespoon salt
600 ml (1 pint) white wine vinegar

(These quantities will give 5 - 6 jars full of pickle)

Cut the pumpkin flesh into small dice. Trim the fennel and chop it into pieces about the same size as the pumpkin.

Put all the ingredients into a preserving pan, bring to the boil and simmer, stirring, until it turns golden brown and shiney - about 20 minutes. Let it cool a little before putting it in the jars.

Store in a cool place for 2 - 3 months before using.

Pumpkin and apple chutney

Unlike most chutneys, this one is a pretty pale cream colour, flecked with red and green from the peppers. Using a distilled malt vinegar instead of the usual brown version, and adding the sultanas at the end, helps to retain this colouring.

8cm (3") fresh ginger root, roughly chopped
12 peppercorns
250 g (8 oz) sultanas
2 kilos (4 lbs) prepared pumpkin
250 g (8 oz) tart apples, e.g Granny Smiths, peeled and cored
250 g (8 oz) onions, chopped
250 g (8 oz) granulated sugar
1 red and 1 green pepper, chopped
900 ml (1 1/2 pints) distilled malt vinegar

(These quantities will give 5 - 6 jars full of chutney)

Put the ginger and peppercorns in a little muslin bag and attach a long string to this. Tie the end to the handle of your preserving pan so that you will be able to remove it easily.

Pour boiling water over the sultanas and leave them to plump up. Chop the pumpkin and apple to small dice.

Put all the ingredients except the sultanas into the preserving pan and bring the mixture up to the boil, then turn the heat down to a fast simmer. Stir frequently until it has thickened and is close to setting point. Drain and add the sultanas, stir them in and cook for a further 5 minutes.

When it is ready, fish out and throw away the bag of ginger and peppercorns before pouring the chutney into the warm jars. Let it cool a little before sealing them.

Pumpkin or squash chutney

Use pumpkin for this recipe and you will get a good sharp chutney. Use squash, and the result will still be sharp, but with an underlying smoothness and rounder flavour. Where many people make chutneys as a way of using up a glut of autumn vegetables, or using up the flesh from a large pumpkin, the squash version of this one is good enough to go out and buy a squash to make it.

---

2 kilos (4 lbs) prepared pumpkin or squash
salt
1 teaspoon whole cloves
1 teaspoon black peppercorns
500 g (1 lb) onions, roughly chopped
2 teaspoons black mustard seed
1 teaspoon powdered ginger
1 teaspoon powdered turmeric
1/2 teaspoon cayenne pepper
1500 ml (2 1/2 pints) malt vinegar
500 g (1 lb) granulated sugar

(This quantity will make 5 - 6 jars of chutney)

Chop the pumpkin into smallish chunks, put these in a bowl and sprinkle them liberally with salt. Leave this overnight to degorge, then rinse well and drain.

Put the cloves and peppercorns in a little muslin bag and attach a long string to this. Tie the end to the handle of your preserving pan so that you will be able to remove it easily.

Put all the ingredients into the preserving pan and bring the mixture up to the boil, then turn the heat down to a fast simmer. Stir frequently until it has thickened and reached setting point.

When it is ready, fish out and throw away the bag of cloves and peppercorns before pouring the chutney into the warm jars. Let it cool a little before sealing them.

Optional variations

• use half pumpkin and half tomatoes.

• add 250 g (8 oz) raisins and/or 250 g (8 oz) chopped walnuts.

• add 2 chopped green peppers.

Pumpkin and onion relish

This relish is what Americans call a 'bread and butter pickle' - (pickle that you eat with bread and butter and cheese or cold meat), which retains a crunchy texture. The cider vinegar gives it an additional piquancy, and the mustard seeds add another dimension to the 'crunch factor'.

12 peppercorns
250 g (8 oz) pearl onions, peeled but whole
2 kilos (4 lbs) prepared pumpkin
100 g (4 oz) granulated sugar
2 teaspoons salt
2 tablespoons white mustard seed
900 ml (1 1/2 pints) apple cider vinegar

(These quantities will give 5 - 6 jars full of relish)

Put the peppercorns in a little muslin bag and attach a long string to this. Tie the end to the handle of your preserving pan so that you will be able to remove it easily. Chop the pumpkin into chunks about the same size as the onions.

Put all the ingredients into the preserving pan and bring the mixture up to the boil, then turn the heat down to simmer for 10 minutes. The pumpkin should be just tender, and the onions still slightly crunchy.

When it is ready, fish out and throw away the bag of peppercorns before pouring the relish into the warm jars. Let it cool a little before sealing them.

Pickled pumpkin

Here is a simple recipe for another sandwich pickle which retains a bitey texture. If you like a strong garlic flavour, chop the cloves into small pieces so that they spread their taste through the pickle. Otherwise, just quarter each clove and leave it to give a subtle hint of flavour.

1 kilo (2 lbs) prepared pumpkin
2 cloves garlic
250 ml (8 fl oz) olive oil
60 ml (2 fl oz) white wine vinegar
4 sprigs fresh thyme or 2 of fresh rosemary

(These quantities will give 2 - 3 jars full of pickle)

Chop the pumpkin into medium sized cubes. Blanch these in boiling water for 3 - 4 minutes, then drain well.

Half fill each jar with pumpkin chunks, then divide the garlic and herbs between the jars before filling them with the rest of the pumpkin chunks. Mix the oil and vinegar and pour this carefully into the jars to cover the pumpkin.

Seal the jars well and store them in a cool place for at least a week, inverting them each day to spread the oil and vinegar evenly.

Baby Pattypans in oil or vinegar

This recipe is really aimed at those who grow their own Pattypan squashes, as they tend to be too expensive to buy in large quantities. But if you do grow your own, you will be delighted to have a recipe that allows you to use up the enormous quantities of baby squashes that even one plant will produce. Use a pretty jar and you have an attractive gift for friends who enjoy delicate flavours, as well as something different to serve with cold meat or pâtés.

Pattypans in vinegar

> **1 kilo (2 lbs) baby Pattypan squash**
> **4 cloves garlic, halved**
> **1 tablespoon salt**
> **1 tablespoon white mustard seeds**
> **4 sprigs fresh thyme**
> **4 fresh sage leaves**
> **1500 ml (2½ pints) white wine vinegar**

Pack Pattypans into jars, divide the garlic, mustard seeds and herbs between the jars, then pour in the vinegar to cover them. Seal the jars and store them in a cool place for 3 - 4 weeks before using.

Tip

- Don't be tempted to heat the vinegar before adding it to the jar, as this tends to make the squashes soggy. (The same applies to pickled onions.)

Pattypans in oil

> **1 kilo (2 lbs) baby Pattypan squash**
> **4 cloves garlic, halved**
> **1 tablespoon salt**
> **4 sprigs fresh thyme or rosemary**
> **4 fresh sage leaves**
> **1500 ml (2¹/₂ pints) olive oil**

Pack Pattypans into jars, divide the garlic and herbs between the jars, then pour in the oil to cover them. Seal the jars and store them in a cool place for 3 - 4 weeks before using.

Cucumber dill pickles

This is an easy recipe for making the classic dilled cucumber pickle. If you grow your own gherkins or ridge cucumbers, you can pick them small enough to stay whole. Otherwise, choose specimens that are no more than 10cm (4") long and cut them in thick diagonal slices.

> **2 kilos (4 lbs) small cucumbers**
> **¹/₂ teaspoon celery seed**
> **¹/₂ teaspoon pickling spice**
> **8 cloves**
> **8cm (3") cinnamon stick**
> **1200 ml (2 pints) apple cider vinegar**
> **1 kilo (2 lbs) granulated sugar**
> **1 teaspoon salt**
> **16 - 24 sprigs of fresh dill**

(These quantities will give 7 - 8 jars full of pickle)

Put the cucumbers in a large bowl or saucepan.

Put the celery seed and spices in a little muslin bag and attach a long string to this. Put the vinegar, sugar and salt into a pan and bring this to the boil, stirring until the sugar has dissolved. Pour the hot liquid over the cucumber and add the bag of spices, tying the string to the handle of the pan so that you will be able to remove it easily. Cover and leave to stand for 24 hours.

Strain the liquid off the cucumbers into a saucepan, add the spice bag and bring this to the boil. Simmer, uncovered, for 30 minutes. Fish out and discard the spice bag.

While the vinegar is simmering, pack the cucumbers into jars and add 2 - 3 sprigs of dill to each jar. When the vinegar is done, pour it over the cucumbers, let them cool for 10 minutes and seal the jars. Store them in a cool place for 3 - 4 weeks before using.

Quick pickled gherkins

This recipe is strictly for the 'grow-it-yourself' brigade, because you need tiny gherkins (sometimes called cornichons), no more than 5cm (2") long. They will keep, in a sealed plastic bag, in the fridge for up to 3 days, which solves the problem of picking them while they are tiny and still having enough to use. This may seem like a bit of a performance, but the end product is crisp crunchy pickled cornichons which you can eat the day after you bottle them.

---

20 - 30 tiny gherkins
2 cloves garlic, quartered
1 large sprig fresh tarragon
225 ml (8 fl oz) white wine vinegar
225 ml (8 fl oz) water
1 teaspoon salt
1 teaspoon sugar

(This quantity makes 1 large jarful)

Pack half the gherkins into a large jar, add the garlic and tarragon and then the rest of the gherkins.

Put the water, vinegar, salt and sugar in a saucepan and bring to the boil, then immediately pour this liquid over the gherkins. Let it cool, cover the jar and leave to stand in a cool place for 12 hours, then in the fridge for at least 2 more hours before serving.

Courgette pickle

This one is for the pickle-loving courgette grower. You can pickle courgettes in any of the ways you would pickle gherkins or cucumbers, but this recipe includes mustard and aniseed to add interest.

---

1 kilo (2 lbs) medium-sized courgettes, thinly sliced
3 small onions, thinly sliced
salt
600 ml (1 pint) distilled malt vinegar
225 g (8 oz) granulated sugar
3 teaspoons powdered mustard
1 teaspoon aniseed
1 teaspoon celery seed

(These quantities will give 5 - 6 jars full of pickle)

Put the sliced courgettes and onions in a wide bowl and sprinkle them liberally with salt. Leave them for an hour to degorge, then rinse them thoroughly and drain them well.

Put all the other ingredients in a saucepan and bring them to the boil, tip in the courgettes and onions, then turn off the heat and let the mixture stand for an hour.

Bring it back to the boil, then simmer for 4 - 5 minutes, let it cool slightly and then bottle it.

Party pumpkin fritters

Serves 12

Ideal for a Hallowe'en party, where you can serve them with other pumpkin based dishes, these fritters are easy to make and will be popular with older guests as well as youngsters. They will taste the same if you just cut them into wedges or squares, but it's more fun if you use shaped biscuit cutters, especially if you can get cutters that follow the Hallowe'en theme.

You can cook them in a shallow layer of oil in a frying pan, but it will be faster, as well as safer, to use a proper deep-fat fryer.

> **1 kilo (2 lbs) prepared pumpkin or squash**
> **250 g (8 oz) plain flour**
> **pinch salt**
> **1 egg**
> **600 ml (1 pint) milk**
> **corn oil for frying**
> **100 g (4 oz) caster sugar**
> **2 teaspoons powdered cinnamon**

Preheat the deep-fat fryer.

Cut the pumpkin into slices no more than 4mm ($^1/_8$") thick, then use biscuit cutters or a sharp knife to cut these into shapes. Set the spare bits aside to make purée for another dish.

Make a thin batter with the flour, salt, egg and milk. Dip the pumpkin pieces into the batter and fry them, a few at a time, until they are golden brown on both sides. Drain well on kitchen paper.

Mix the sugar and cinnamon, and toss the cooked fritters in it to coat well on both sides. Serve while they are still hot.

Squash pancakes

They may be fattening, but no-one can resist pancakes. Adding squash to your batter makes luscious pancakes with a taste that is almost addictive. I had the builders in the house when I was working on this recipe, and being a cook who never misses a chance to get a third or more opinions on my experiments, I tried these pancakes on the plasterer and his mate. They thought the pancakes were wonderful - and repaid me by bringing me a hot sausage sandwich for my breakfast the next day.

Any of the winter squashes give a good result, but for the best flavour, use Acorn, Delicata or Sweet Dumpling.

> **250 g (8 oz) plain flour**
> **pinch salt**
> **1 egg**
> **250 g (8 oz) squash purée**
> **600 ml (1 pint) milk**
> **butter for frying**
> **caster sugar**
> **lemon juice**

Start making the batter in the usual way, by putting the egg into the flour and salt, then add the squash purée and mix it in. Continue by adding the milk a little at a time, stirring well to avoid lumps. Add as much milk as is needed to produce the consistency of batter you prefer. You may not need all the milk. Leave the batter to stand for at least 30 minutes.

Heat a frying pan and melt a little butter in it, then pour in a tablespoon of batter. It is best to make small pancakes, as this batter gives a very soft result. Wait for about 30 seconds, then see if the pancake is ready to turn by lifting it with a spatula. Turn it and cook the other side for another 30 seconds.

When it is cooked, turn it onto a plate and repeat the procedure as many times as necessary.

Serve the pancakes with caster sugar and lemon juice for diners to add to their own taste. If you're feeling in need of a treat, substitute Grand Marnier for the lemon juice!

Squash baked pancake with stewed plums

Having discovered how delicious squash pancakes are, I then wondered about using the same batter to make a clafouti - that French baked dessert made with a sweet batter containing fruit. A classic clafouti is made with black cherries, but I was experimenting in winter, and all I had available was some plums in the freezer. I wasn't sure how the plums would behave - I worried that they might make the batter round them soggy - so I baked the batter on its own and added the plums afterwards. It was a great success, and has become part of our standard repertoire.

---

250 g (8 oz) plain flour
pinch salt
1 egg
250 g (8 oz) squash purée
2 tablespoons caster sugar
600 ml (1 pint) milk
1 kilo (2 lbs) plums, stoned
100 g (4 oz) sugar
200 ml (6 fl oz) whipping cream

Preheat the oven to 325°F (160°C) Gas Mark 3 and butter an ovenproof dish.

Start making the batter in the usual way, by putting the egg into the flour and salt, then add the squash purée and mix it in. Stir in the sugar. Continue by adding the milk a little at a time, stirring well to avoid lumps. This batter needs to be slightly thicker than pancake batter, so you may not need all the milk. Leave the batter to stand for at least 30 minutes before proceeding.

Pour the batter into the buttered dish and bake it for 30 - 40 minutes, until a skewer comes out clean.

Meanwhile, cook the plums and sugar over a gentle heat. When they are soft, check to see if they are sweet enough and add more sugar if necessary. Whip the cream to soft peaks.

Serve the pudding in slices, with some stewed plums and a dollop of cream. Take some caster sugar to the table for those diners who like their plums really sweet.

Optional variations

• Omit the plums and serve with sugar and lime juice or Grand Marnier.

Squash and prune tart

Is it a pie or is it a tart? American pumpkin pie has an open top, but in the UK pie usually means closed top. This one has an open top, and I've decided to call it a tart. Whatever you call it, it is an interesting marriage of flavours which come out best if you serve it hot. The cream in the filling gives a surface that looks rather like crème brûlée, and you need to watch it carefully in the final stage of cooking so that it doesn't go too far and burn.

---

enough short crust pastry to line a 23cm (9") flan dish
8 - 10 presoaked stoneless prunes
250 g (8 oz) squash purée
50 g (2 oz) sugar
2 eggs, beaten
150 ml (5 fl oz) double cream

Preheat the oven to 325°F (160°C) Gas Mark 3.

Grease a flan dish and line it with the pastry. Roughly cut the prunes into quarters and spread these out on the bottom of the pastry.

Mix together the squash purée, sugar, eggs and cream, and pour this mixture over the prunes. With a fork, loosen the prunes a little so that the mixture can get underneath them, but covers them completely.

Paint the exposed parts of pastry with egg-yolk or milk before putting the tart in the oven. Bake it for 50 - 60 minutes, checking it after 20 and 40 minutes to make sure it doesn't burn. If it looks as though it might, lay a sheet of foil over the top until 10 minutes before the end of cooking, then take this off to brown the top.

If possible, turn off the oven and leave the tart inside for 15 minutes before taking it out. Otherwise, pop it back in for 5 - 10 minutes to warm through before serving.

Classic American pumpkin pie

Serves 6 -8

This is the definitive recipe for the kind of pumpkin pie that is traditionally served in America for Thanksgiving dinner. It is very rich and full of spices, so serve it in small slices.

---

enough short crust pastry to line a 23 cm (9") flan dish
300 g (12 oz) pumpkin purée
325 ml (12 fl oz) double cream
8 level tablespoons light brown sugar
1/2 teaspoon salt
1 teaspoon powdered cinnamon
1/2 teaspoon powdered ginger
a generous pinch ground cloves
120 ml (4 fl oz) golden syrup
3 eggs, beaten
1 teaspoon vanilla extract
whipped cream for serving

Preheat the oven to 325°F (160°C) Gas Mark 3.

Grease a flan dish and line it with the pastry.

Mix all the ingredients, except the whipped cream, thoroughly and pour them into the pastry.

Paint the exposed parts of pastry with egg-yolk or milk before putting the tart in the oven. Bake it for 50 - 60 minutes, checking it after 20 and 40 minutes to make sure it doesn't burn. If it looks as though it might, lay a sheet of foil over the top until 10 minutes before the end of cooking, then take this off to brown the top.

When it is ready, take it out of the oven and leave it to cool completely. Whip the cream and either pipe rosettes on top of the filling, or hand it separately when serving.

Optional variations

- omit the vanilla extract and use 2 tablespoons brandy or rum.
- add 1 tablespoon chopped preserved ginger.
- add 50 g (2 oz) coarsely chopped walnuts, sprinkling these over the top before baking.
- add 50 g (2 oz) pecan nut halves, laying these carefully on top of the filling before baking.

Pumpkin chiffon pie

Some people find the classic American pumpkin pie over-spiced and rather heavy. If you're one of them, this is the version for you - much lighter, both in spices and texture.

250 g (8 oz) ginger biscuits, crumbed
100g (4 oz) butter, melted
1 sachet gelatine
2 tablespoons warm water
4 eggs, separated
500 g (1 lb) pumpkin purée
150 g (6 oz) granulated sugar
120 ml (4 fl oz) double cream
1/2 teaspoon powdered ginger
1/2 teaspoon powdered cinnamon
1/4 teaspoon grated nutmeg

Preheat the oven to 375°F (190°C) Gas Mark 5.

Mix the biscuit crumbs and butter and press the mixture onto the base of a 20 cm (9") flan dish. Bake this for 8 minutes and let it cool.

Dissolve the gelatine in the warm water. Beat the egg whites into stiff peaks.

Combine the gelatine with the pumpkin purée and two thirds of the sugar.

Put this mixture into a saucepan with the yolks of the eggs, the cream and the spices, and cook, stirring constantly, until it is thick. Let it cool slightly, then stir in the rest of the sugar and fold in the egg whites.

Pour this mixture into the dish on top of the biscuit crust and put the dish into a cool place to set. This should take 2 - 3 hours. You can move it into the fridge once it is cool.

Optional variation

- Whisk 120 ml (4 fl oz) whipping cream with 1 teaspoon of icing sugar and pipe this in rosettes on top of the filling once it has cooled down.

Squash and raisin buns

This recipe gives the sort of bun that Americans call a muffin, so you will need the larger size of bun papers. Whatever you call it, the end result is a light textured and spicy bun that is excellent eaten cold, but even better when eaten warm. I like them warm with butter and jam, but those additions are not compulsory if you're diet-conscious!

---

300 g (10 oz) self raising flour
1 teaspoon baking powder
1/2 teaspoon salt
1/4 teaspoon powdered cinnamon
1/4 teaspoon grated nutmeg
75 g (2 1/2 oz) light brown sugar
150 g (5 oz) raisins
175 g (7 oz) squash purée
2 eggs, beaten
120 ml (4 fl oz) milk
50 g (2 oz) butter, melted

Preheat the oven to 400°F (200°C) Gas Mark 6. Set out 12 paper bun cups on a baking tray.

Sift together the flour, baking powder, salt, and spices, then stir in the sugar and raisins.

In a separate bowl, mix together the squash purée, eggs, milk and melted butter, then fold this mixture into the dry ingredients to make a loose batter.

Divide the batter between 12 paper bun cups, filling each about two thirds full. Bake in the middle of the oven for 25 - 30 minutes, when they should be golden brown and a skewer comes out clean. Leave them on the baking tray for 1 -2 minutes, then transfer them to a wire tray to finish cooling.

Optional variations

● omit the raisins and cinnamon, and substitute 100 g (4 oz) grated Parmesan cheese. (You can also add some chopped chives if you like.)

● add 2 tablespoons orange juice and 2 teaspoons finely chopped orange zest.

Squash scones

These scones are just as easy to make as the simple ones that everyone learns in school cookery classes. The difference is that with squash purée added to the other ingredients not only is the flavour enhanced but the end result is a rich golden colour right through. Eat them with butter and jam - any sort of jam, but particularly one of the pumpkin or squash jams in this book.

---

100 g (4 oz) self raising flour
2 teaspoons baking powder
pinch salt
50 g (2 oz) butter
100 g (4 oz) squash purée
milk to mix

Preheat the oven to 475°F (240°C) Gas Mark 9 and prepare a baking tray by dusting it lightly with flour.

Sift the dry ingredients into a mixing bowl and mix in the squash purée, then add sufficient milk to make a light dough.

Turn the dough out of the bowl onto a floured surface and roll it out gently to about 5cm (2") thick. The less you handle this dough, the better. Cut out rounds with a pastry cutter or other shapes using a knife, then place each piece on the baking sheet, leaving a little space between them.

Brush the tops with milk. Bake the scones for 12 - 15 minutes, then space them out on a wire rack to cool.

Optional variations

- sprinkle some sesame seeds on top of the scones after brushing them with milk.

- add 1 tablespoon of chopped fresh herbs to the mixture with the purée, then 50 g (2 oz) grated cheese.

Squash noodles with apricot cream sauce

Most people are so used to thinking of pasta as being a savoury dish that they are surprised when you suggest it can also be a sweet. I have a number of recipes for sweet pasta dishes, so it wasn't long after I started making squash pasta before I started thinking of sweet sauces that would enhance its delicate flavour. This recipe works perfectly well if you use the squashes I suggest on pages 8-9, but it is even better if you use Delicata, Sweet Dumpling or Acorn.

The orange flower water isn't essential, but it adds another dimension and takes the edge off what might otherwise be excessive sweetness.

---

1 recipe of squash pasta, cut into thin noodles (page 37)
1 - 2 tablespoons granulated sugar
20 dried apricots
3 tablespoons boiling water
250 ml (8 fl oz) double cream
1 - 2 tablespoons orange flower water
nutmeg

Sprinkle the sugar over the apricots, then add the boiling water and leave them to soften completely - about 1 hour. Whizz them in a food processor or liquidizer to a coarse purée.

Transfer the purée to a saucepan, and over a cool heat gradually stir in the cream, taking care that it does not separate. If it shows signs of doing this, stir in a sprinkle of plain flour. Finally stir in the orange flower water.

Meanwhile cook and drain the pasta. Toss the pasta in the sauce to heat it through before serving with a grating of nutmeg on top.

Lemon pumpkin pie

Many years ago, a friend who doesn't like the heavily spiced version of pumpkin pie announced that she had found a recipe for a lemon version. The individual drupelets of lemon were still intact, and released their juice as you bit into them. It was wonderful, but like a fool I didn't get the recipe from her before she moved away and we lost contact. It took me a lot of experimenting to come up with the version below, but I finally got it right.

If you don't have the time or patience to separate the drupelets out, it does work with lemon juice alone, but the final result isn't quite the same. You may need more or less sugar, depending on the sweetness of the lemons, and your personal taste.

---

enough short crust pastry to line a 23cm (9") flan dish
2 large lemons
125 g (5 oz) caster sugar
2 eggs, beaten
500 g (1 lb) pumpkin purée

Preheat the oven to 375°F (190°C) Gas Mark 5.

Grease a flan dish and line it with the pastry.

Wipe the lemons and with a zester, scrape off all the zest into a mixing bowl. Then half the lemons across their waist, and standing them on a cutting board, use a very sharp knife to remove the outer skin and the skin of the inner segments. Then slide the knife down the skin of each segment and pull out the flesh. Remove any pips and gently pull the drupelets apart so that as many as possible remain intact. Do this over the bowl so that you retain any stray juice. If you find this performance too much for you, just squeeze out the juice instead.

Add half the sugar, taste, and add more sugar until the result is sweet enough for you before mixing in the eggs and pumpkin purée.

Pour the mixture into the prepared pastry case and bake for 35 - 40 minutes, checking regularly to ensure that the top doesn't burn. If this seems imminent, arrange a piece of cooking foil over the top.

Serve hot or cold.

Elderflower pumpkin pie

You can buy elderflower syrup at health food shops, but it is very easy to make your own, so I've given you the recipe on page 163. I always have a bottle in my cupboard, so when I was looking for new things to do with pumpkin purée, it wasn't long before I wondered if the two would combine to make a sweet tart. They did, and you can try the result for yourself.

---

enough short crust pastry to line a 23cm (9") flan dish
2 eggs, separated
500 g (1 lb) pumpkin purée
6 tablespoons elderflower syrup
4 tablespoons self raising flour

Preheat the oven to 350°F (180°C) Gas Mark 4.

Grease a flan dish and line it with the pastry.

Whip the egg whites to soft peaks. Mix the egg yolks, pumpkin purée, syrup and flour to a smooth batter, then gently fold in the egg whites.

Pour the mixture into the prepared pastry case and bake for 35 - 40 minutes, checking regularly to ensure that the top doesn't burn. If this seems imminent, arrange a piece of cooking foil over the top.

Serve hot or cold.

Crisp squash and orange biscuits

I started experimenting with these biscuits just before Hallowe'en and the first batch were sort of pumpkin shaped with icing on top. But there was a little bit of the dough left, so I rolled it out very thin and just marked it into squares before I baked it. I managed to taste a couple of them and thought that I preferred the thin plain version to the thicker iced version - but before I had a chance to try another one, the Hallowe'en spirits seemed to have passed through my kitchen, leaving nothing but a few crumbs!

Whichever version you make, if you do it for Hallowe'en, the end result is more fun if you use a set of cutters that produce appropriate shapes - cats, witches hats or what-have-you.

---

325 g (13 oz) plain flour
¼ teaspoon ground cinnamon
¼ teaspoon ground ginger
¼ teaspoon grated nutmeg
pinch salt
150 g (6 oz) softened butter
50 g (2 oz) light brown sugar
1 tablespoon peel-free marmalade,
   or pumpkin and orange jam (page 100)
150 g (6 oz) squash purée - any of the golden-fleshed
   varieties
1 egg yolk

Preheat the oven to 400°F (200°C) Gas Mark 6 and grease 2 baking sheets.

Sift the flour, spices and salt together in a bowl. In a separate bowl, cream together the butter and sugar until they are pale and soft. Beat in the squash purée and egg yolk, then add this mixture to the flour and mix it to a soft dough. Roll this into a ball and pop it into a plastic bag before leaving it to rest for at least 30 minutes in the fridge.

Roll the dough out, cut it with biscuit cutters or a knife, and lay the shapes on the baking tray.

For thick biscuits, roll the dough to about 5mm (¼") thick and bake for 8 - 10 minutes.

For thin biscuits, roll the dough to about 3mm (⅛") thick and bake for 5 - 6 minutes.

Icing

> **500 g (1 lb) icing sugar**
> **4 egg whites**
> **1 tablespoon orange juice**
> **food colouring (orange and black)**

Sift the icing sugar into a bowl and beat in the egg whites and orange juice. If you are making cat or witches' hat shapes, add 2 - 4 drops of black colouring, otherwise add 2 - 4 drops of orange colouring. (Or put some of the icing in a separate bowl and make batches of separate colours.) Smooth the icing over the biscuits, adding appropriate features in the contrasting colour.

Delicata Bavarian cream

Serves 8 - 10

This is a very rich pudding, so serve it in small portions. Brave cooks might like to make it in a mould and turn it out. Less brave ones, (like me), can make it in small ramekins and serve one to each diner. It needs a sharp fruit sauce to go with it, such as a raspberry or strawberry coulis, (see page 165) which you can either pour over or round the demoulded version, or on top of each ramekin.

If you can't get Delicata squash, use Acorn or Sweet Dumpling.

> **250 g (8 oz) squash purée**
> **50 g (2 oz) caster sugar**
> **10 g (1/2 oz) butter**
> **1/2 sachet gelatin**
> **150 ml (5 fl oz) whipping cream**
> **2 drops vanilla essence**

Heat the squash purée with half the sugar and the butter, then sprinkle the gelatine over the top and stir it in. Leave to cool.

Meanwhile, whip the cream, the rest of the sugar and the vanilla together, to the soft peak stage.

Gently fold the whipped cream into the purée mixture and then pour the mixture into the final dish or dishes. Put it into the fridge to set and chill for at least 3 hours.

Squash cheesecake

Serves 8 - 10

This is a baked cheesecake. Although it is very rich, that richness is offset by the lime juice, and the strips of lime zest on the top contrast nicely with the orangey-cream of the filling. To make it easier to get the finished cake out of the baking tin, it is best to use a spring-clip pan. Any of the firmer-fleshed squashes will do for this recipe, but Delicata or Sweet Dumpling will give the tastiest result.

---

250 g (8 oz) digestive biscuits, crushed
100 g (4 oz) butter, melted
2 tablespoons light brown sugar
zest from 1 lime
3 tablespoons water
4 tablespoons caster sugar
250 ml (8 fl oz) double cream
250 g (8 oz) cream cheese
3 eggs, beaten
2 tablespoons plain flour, sifted
250 g (8 oz) squash purée
1 tablespoon fresh lime juice

Preheat the oven to 375°F (190°C) Gas Mark 5. Grease a spring-clip cake tin.

Mix the crushed biscuits with the melted butter and light brown sugar, then press this mix into the bottom and sides of the cake tin. Bake for 8 - 10 minutes and leave to cool.

Put the lime zest in a small saucepan with the water and 2 tablespoons of the caster sugar. Bring to the boil and simmer for 4 - 5 minutes. Drain the zest and leave it to cool.

Stir 2 tablespoons of the caster sugar into the double cream until the sugar has dissolved. Leave this to stand.

Soften the cream cheese and beat in the eggs, flour, squash purée and lime juice. Pour this mixture into the cake tin on top of the base, and bake until almost set - 40 - 45 minutes. Take it out of the oven, spoon the cream and sugar mixture over the top and return it to the oven for 5 minutes.

Take it out of the oven and leaving it in the tin, let it cool completely before putting it in the fridge to chill for at least 12 hours.

Decorate the top with the lime zest before serving.

Optional variation

- omit the lime juice, replacing it with 1 - 2 tablespoons of pumpkin and orange jam (see page100).

Orange squash charlotte

Serves 8 - 10

This is a very rich charlotte, and should be served in small portions. I should warn you that you will need at least 6 mixing bowls for the different parts of the filling, but the end result more than compensates for the washing up.

Incidentally, the diet-conscious can substitute sieved cottage cheese for the cream cheese, and yoghurt for some of the cream.

---

1 packet boudoir biscuits
2 - 3 tablespoons Grand Marnier
3 eggs, separated
75 g (3 oz) caster sugar
250 g (8 oz) cream cheese
250 g (8 oz) squash purée
1 orange jelly
240 ml (8 fl oz) double cream

Spread the biscuits out, sugar side down, on a tray and sprinkle them with the Grand Marnier.

Fill a bowl with hot water and put another bowl into it. In this second bowl, whisk together the egg yolks and the caster sugar until they are pale and have thickened. In another bowl, or in a food processor, beat together the cream cheese and squash purée. In a fourth bowl whisk the egg whites to the stiff peaks stage. In another bowl (I did warn you this needs a lot of bowls) whisk the cream to soft peaks. In a final bowl, melt the jelly with 3 - 4 tablespoons boiling water. This can be done by giving it 1 minute on High in the microwave.

Stand the biscuits up, sugar side out, in your dish. (This needs to be a deep-sided dish about 20cm (8") across - if you intend to turn the charlotte out, a spring-clip cake tin is ideal, otherwise use a soufflé dish.) To ensure that the biscuits stay in place, dip the end of each one in the whipped cream for the filling and use this to 'glue' it in place.

Now assemble the various mixtures. Beat the egg yolk mixture into the squash and cheese mixture, then stir in the jelly. Fold in the whipped cream and finally the egg whites before pouring the mixture into your prepared dish. Put the charlotte in the fridge to set and chill for at least 6 hours before serving.

* This dish contains uncooked eggs, and thus should not be given to the very young, the very old, the ill, pregnant women, or anyone else likely to be vulnerable to salmonella.

Connie's pumpkin charlotte

Serves 8 - 10

Connie Berto is a very dear American friend of mine, who sent me this recipe to try when I mentioned I was doing this book. The end result is rather like a creamy version of the classic spicy pumpkin pie.

---

1 packet boudoir biscuits
250 ml (8 fl oz) rum
2 sachets gelatine
150 ml (5 fl oz) milk
4 eggs, separated
150 g (6 oz) light brown sugar
500 g (1 lb) pumpkin purée
1 1/2 teaspoons ground cinnamon
1/2 teaspoon salt
1/2 teaspoon ground allspice
1/2 teaspoon ground ginger
1/2 teaspoon grated nutmeg
50 g (2 oz) walnuts, chopped
250 ml (8 fl oz) double cream

Spread the biscuits out, sugar side down, on a tray and sprinkle them with 2 - 3 tablespoons of the rum. In a saucepan over a low heat, beat together the gelatine, milk, the rest of the rum, the egg yolks and half the sugar, until they form a soft custard. Take the pan off the heat and stir in the pumpkin purée, salt and spices. Leave it to cool.

Whisk the cream to soft peaks.

Stand the boudoir biscuits up, sugar side out, in your dish. (This needs to be a deep-sided dish about 20cm (8") across - if you intend to turn the charlotte out, a spring-clip cake tin is ideal, otherwise use a soufflé dish.) To ensure that the biscuits stay in place, dip the end of each one in the whipped cream for the filling and use this to 'glue' it in place. Sprinkle the chopped walnuts over the bottom of the dish.

Whisk the egg whites and the rest of the sugar to stiff peaks. Fold the cream into the pumpkin custard, then fold the egg whites into that. Pour the mixture into the prepared dish and put it in the fridge to set and chill for at least 6 hours before turning it out.

* This dish contains uncooked eggs, and thus should not be given to the very young, the very old, the ill, pregnant women, or anyone else likely to be vulnerable to salmonella.

Crystallised squash

This is a jelly-like sweet, which you can bring out to accompany the coffee at the end of a meal, or package up as gifts. The method is easy enough, just requiring the patience to repeat the process several times until the consistency is right.

You can use any type of squash or pumpkin for this recipe, as long as it gives you reasonable sized slices.

---

1 kilo (2 lbs) prepared squash flesh
650 g (1 lb 6 oz) granulated sugar
500 g (1 lb) light brown sugar
juice of 1 lemon
water
1 sachet gelatine
a little oil
150 g (6 oz) icing sugar

Slice the squash and cut it into suitable shapes, such as diamonds. Sprinkle it with 150 g (6 oz) of the granulated sugar and leave it to degorge for several hours. Rinse, drain and dry.

Oil a baking tray and set it aside. Preheat the oven to its lowest setting.

Put the rest of the granulated sugar and the brown sugar in a saucepan with the lemon juice and bring it to the boil, adding only just enough water to make it liquid. Add the gelatine, then the squash and move it around gently to ensure it is covered with the syrup. Cook gently for 5 minutes.

Draw the pan off the heat and take the squash pieces out of the syrup with a slotted spoon, then lay them on the oiled tray so that they do not touch each other. Retain the syrup. Dry them in the oven for 5 - 6 hours, let them cool and chill them in the fridge for 12 hours.

Bring the syrup back to the boil, put the squash pieces in and cook them gently for 5 minutes, dry and chill as before. Repeat this process 3 or 4 times, until the pieces have a firm jelly-like texture. Sprinkle them with sifted icing sugar and store in an airtight box.

Delicata and apple flan

This is a variation on the French-style apple tarts where slices of apples are arranged on top of either plain pastry or a custardy base. Here, the custard has been replaced by a layer of squash purée, which softens the sharpness of the apple without being too sweet.

Delicata or Sweet Dumpling squash are best for this recipe, but Acorn would do.

---

enough short-crust pastry to line a 23cm (9") flan dish
250 g (8 oz) squash purée
3 sharp apples, such as Granny Smith
a few drops of lemon juice in a dish of water
2 tablespoons apricot jam
milk or egg yolk to glaze the pastry

Preheat the oven to 425°F (220°C) Gas Mark 7.

Use the pastry to line the dish, and prick it with a fork in the middle to prevent it rising during cooking.

Spread the squash purée evenly over the pastry.

Quarter and de-core the apples, but do not peel them. Slice them thinly, dropping each piece in the lemon juice water as you work. This stops the apple discolouring. When all the apples are ready, arrange them on top of the squash purée. The traditional way to arrange them is in concentric rings, with the slices over-lapping. (If one of your apples has red skin, you could use these slices to make a prettier pattern.)

Add a little boiling water to the apricot jam and paint it over the apple slices. Paint the visible surfaces of pastry with egg yolk or milk before baking the flan for 25 - 30 minutes.

Serve hot or cold.

Optional variations

- soak 50 g (2 oz) sultanas in 2 tablespoons Calvados until they have plumped up. Sprinkle them over the squash purée before adding the apple slices.
- alternate slices of raw squash with slices of apple.

Spicy squash cake with date and walnut

Serves 8 - 10

This is a very filling cake, ideal for accompanying your morning coffee if you missed breakfast. Heavy with chopped dates, and with the additional crunch of chopped walnuts, it's full of energy-giving ingredients, and it should keep you going until dinner time.

Use any squash or pumpkin, but be prepared to adjust the moisture content if your squash is dry-fleshed.

---

400 g (13 oz) self raising flour
1/2 teaspoon grated nutmeg
3/4 teaspoon ground cinnamon
1/2 teaspoon ground allspice
1/2 teaspoon salt
250 g (8 oz) butter, softened
250 g (8 oz) light brown sugar
2 large eggs
250 g (8 oz) squash purée
1 teaspoon vanilla essence
125 g (5 oz) dried dates, soaked and coarsely chopped
125 g (5 oz) walnuts, chopped
120 ml (4 fl oz) milk

Preheat the oven to 350°F (180°C) Gas Mark 4. Grease a square baking tin, approximately 32 by 23 by 5cm (13 by 9 by 2").

Sift the flour, spices and salt into a mixing bowl. Cream the butter and sugar together until they are creamy, then beat in the eggs, one at a time.

Beat in the squash purée and the vanilla, then pour this mixture into the flour and stir well. Stir in the dates and walnuts, then sufficient milk to make a fairly stiff batter. Pour this into the prepared baking tin, smooth it into the corners and bake for 55 - 60 minutes, until a skewer comes out clean.

Leave it to cool for about 10 minutes in the tin before turning it out onto a wire rack to cool completely.

Squash tart with nuts and raisins

Serves 8 - 10

This is a spicy tart, with contrasting textures of juicy raisins and crunchy walnuts to offset the smoothness of the custardy base. If you want an extra dimension of crunch, you can add some flaked almonds on top, but you have to be careful they don't burn. A piece of cooking foil, laid over the top of the dish, is my saviour every time in this situation.

Use an Acorn squash for this dish, or if you make it in the summer, use courgettes.

---

enough short-crust pastry to line a 23cm (9") flan dish
250 g (8 oz) squash flesh, grated
1/2 teaspoon ground cinnamon
1/4 teaspoon ground ginger
75 g (3 oz) light brown sugar
3 eggs, beaten
175 g (6 oz) crème fraîche or thick yoghurt
50 g (2 oz) raisins, plumped in hot water
50 g (2 oz) walnuts, coarsely chopped
25 g (1 oz) flaked almonds (optional)

Preheat the oven to 350°F (180°C) Gas Mark 4. Line the flan dish with the pastry and prick the bottom so that it doesn't rise during cooking.

Beat the spices and sugar into the purée, then beat in the eggs. Beat the crème fraîche a little to soften it before beating it into the squash mixture, then stir in the raisins and walnuts. Pour this mixture into the prepared dish and level it off. If using the flaked almonds, scatter them over the top of the filling.

Bake for 55 - 60 minutes until the filling is set and a skewer comes out clean.

Serve warm or cold.

Pumpkin and almond tart

Serves 8

The 'patronne' in our favourite Provencal hotel raided our car when we turned up one year with a bootful of squash and pumpkins which we had acquired at a pumpkin fair en route. By the time we got down to the dining room that evening, she had created a wonderful display of squash on one of the side tables, and a squash and tomato gratin had been added to the menu. Then she told us about this tart, which is a traditional Christmas dish in Provence, so of course I had to try it as soon as I got home. You don't have to wait until Christmas to try it for yourself - it's delicious any time.

**enough short crust pastry to line a 23cm (9") pie dish,
and some spare to make the lattice
350 g (12 oz) pumpkin purée
100 g (4 oz) ground almonds
100 g (4 oz) caster sugar
1 teaspoon orange flower water
1 tablespoon lemon zest
a little milk for glazing the pastry**

Preheat the oven to 425°F (220°C) Gas Mark 7. Line the pie dish with pastry, then roll out the rest of the pastry and cut it into thin strips.

Beat the ground almonds, sugar, lemon zest and orange flower water into the pumpkin purée and pour it into the prepared dish. Use the strips of spare pastry to weave a lattice covering, sticking it down at each side with milk. Brush the lattice and edges of the pie with milk before baking it for 35 minutes.

Serve warm or cold.

Sweet pumpkin omelette

This is a fluffy omelette with sweetened pumpkin cubes inside and a wickedly alcoholic apple sauce on top. The only snag about it is that the cook has to disappear into the kitchen to make it, leaving the other diners at the table. In an ideal world, we'd all have kitchens big enough to include the dining table.

---

75 g (3 oz) prepared pumpkin flesh, in small cubes
150 g (6 oz) caster sugar
6 eggs, separated
unsalted butter for the omelette pan
150 g (6 oz) apple purée
3 - 4 tablespoons Calvados
icing sugar

Put the pumpkin cubes in a saucepan with one third of the sugar and just enough water to cover them. Poach for about 5 minutes, until the pumpkin is tender but not collapsing. Lift the cubes out of the syrup with a slotted spoon and leave them to drain.

Beat the egg whites with another third of the sugar to the stiff peaks stage. Beat the egg yolks, then fold in the whites. Melt a little butter in your omelette pan and make either one large or four small omelettes, putting the pumpkin cubes in the middle before folding each omelette.

Meanwhile, put the remaining sugar into the apple purée and heat it gently until the sugar has dissolved. Just before serving, stir in the Calvados and spoon the sauce over the omelettes.

Sift some icing sugar on top of the omelettes before serving.

Caramelised Butternut squash with an orange sauce

This is a dish that takes advantage of the solid piece of flesh on a Butternut squash, as you can slice it into neat rondels. You could also use Acorn squash, cut into rings, but there is a risk that they would fall apart as you lift them from the pan. But if you're not too concerned about the look of the finished dish, you could make it with slices of any of the sweeter fleshed squash.

---

1 medium sized Butternut squash
4 tablespoons light brown sugar
unsalted butter for frying
3 large navel oranges
2 tablespoons of Cointreau
4 sprigs of mint for garnishing

Cut the bell end off the squash and save it for another dish. Peel the straight end and slice it into 8 rondels about 1cm (½") thick. Lay these in a wide dish and sprinkle the sugar over them. Leave this to macerate for about 30 minutes before frying them both sides in butter until they are tender. Take the pan off the heat and lift out the rondels with a slotted spoon and put them on a spare dish.

With a lemon zester, pare some strips of zest from two of the oranges. Working over a bowl to catch the juice, remove all the peel and pith with a sharp knife, taking off the inside skin as well. Cut between the skin of each segment to remove the contents. Squeeze the juice from the third orange.

Put the pan back on the heat and fry the orange segments for 2 - 3 minutes. Add the juice and then the Cointreau and stir gently until it is hot. Finally put the squash rondels back in the pan and move them around gently until they have heated right through.

Serve decorated with a sprig of mint.

Optional variation

- add a few sliced kumquats to the sauce.

Coconut custard in squash shells

For this dish you need smallish green or golden coloured squash, such as Gold Nugget or Kabocha. The custard is baked in the squash shells, then chilled until it will cut cleanly, so you serve two squash quarters to each diner.

---

200 g block creamed coconut
150 ml (5 fl oz) boiling water
4 large eggs, beaten
100 g (4 oz) granulated sugar
2 small squash, prepared for stuffing
1 tablespoon rose water (optional)
toasted coconut swirls to garnish

Preheat the oven to 300°F (150°C) Gas Mark 2.

Roughly chop the coconut cream and put it in a bowl with the boiling water to melt.

Beat the sugar and rosewater into the eggs, then beat in the coconut liquid. Stand the prepared squash in a deep baking tray and pour the custard into them, then replace the 'lids'.

Pour enough boiling water into the dish to come about half-way up the sides of the squash and bake them for about 75 minutes, until the custard has set. Move the squash from the baking tin to another dish and let them cool completely before putting them in the fridge to chill for at least 3 hours.

When you are ready to serve them, remove the lids and with a very sharp knife cut each squash into quarters from the top down. Give each diner two quarters, garnishing the dish with some swirls of toasted coconut.

Butternut squash and rum brûlée

A simple variation on crème brûlée, this dish combines the smooth unctuousness of the crème base with the sharp crunchiness of the caramelised sugar topping. Unlike some brûlées, which include egg yolk and have to be baked first, this one just needs the ingredients to be folded together before chilling - so all you have to do at serving time is the magic trick with the sugar and the grill.

**2 tablespoons rum
150 g (6 oz) light brown sugar
250 g (8 oz) Butternut squash purée
300 ml (10 fl oz) whipping cream
nutmeg**

Beat the rum and two-thirds of the sugar into the squash purée, then put this mixture into your serving dish - either one large dish or 4 medium sized ramekins.

Whip the cream very stiff, and pack this on top of the squash. Chill in the fridge for several hours - the colder the cream is when you come to melt the sugar, the less likely the cream is to melt, and the quicker the sugar will set into a solid sheet of almost-toffee.

When you are ready to serve it, grate plenty of nutmeg over the cream, then sprinkle on the rest of the sugar, ensuring that all the cream is covered. Now, if you have a salamander, you can use that, or if you feel brave enough to use a blow-torch, use that to melt the sugar. Otherwise, preheat the grill until it is glowing, and pop the dish underneath it. Don't leave it - watch it, turning the dish if necessary to ensure all the sugar is melted, then take it out from the grill and take it to the table.

Delicata squash ice-cream

This is a rich ice-cream, made with real cream, but unlike some other ice-creams where you have to cook the base custard, all you have to do to make this one is to whip this and that, then fold it together before freezing.

It really should be made with Delicata or Sweet Dumpling squash for the full flavour, but Acorn would be an acceptable substitute.

**yolks of 2 large eggs
100 g (4 oz) caster sugar
250 g (8 oz) squash purée
200 ml (7 fl oz) whipping cream
5 - 6 drops of vanilla essence**

Beat the egg yolks with half the sugar until they are pale and creamy, and leave a trail across the surface when you lift the whisk. Stir in the squash purée and mix well.

Beat the cream with the rest of the sugar until it is quite stiff, then fold it into the squash mixture.

If you have an ice-cream machine, put the mixture in and let the machine get on with it. Otherwise, spread the mixture evenly in a wide flat dish (I use a small baking tray) and put it in the freezer. Leave it for about 3 hours, then take it out and beat it with a fork to break up the ice crystals and soften it up, then put it back to freeze for another 2 hours, after which you can serve it.

If you want to keep it longer, transfer it to a more appropriate container and return it to the freezer. Allow it to soften in the fridge for about 30 minutes before serving.

Optional variation

- add 50 g (2 oz) finely chopped walnuts before freezing.
- This dish contains uncooked eggs, and thus should not be given to the very young, the very old, the ill, pregnant women, or anyone else likely to be vulnerable to salmonella.

Spicy pumpkin rum and raisin ice cream

I've tried a number of versions of spicy pumpkin ice-cream, which to my mind are very little different from the classic pumpkin pie. After some experimentation, I came up with my own version, less heavy in the spice department but with rum-soaked raisins to add an extra dimension to it. You'll need to set the raisins soaking at least 12 hours before you start making the ice cream, or you may like to add rum-soaked raisins to your store-cupboard stand-by list - I always have a bottle of them lurking in the cupboard, and they get used for all sorts of things, not least of which is bread-and-butter pudding.

For this recipe, the pumpkin purée should be run through a food-processor or liquidizer to remove any trace of granularity.

50 g (2 oz) raisins
3 tablespoons dark rum
yolks of 2 eggs
3 tablespoons caster sugar
200 ml (7 fl oz) milk
1/2 teaspoon ground ginger
1/2 teaspoon ground cinnamon
1/4 teaspoon ground allspice
500 g (1 lb) pumpkin or squash purée
200 ml (7 fl oz) whipping cream

Put the raisins and the rum in a small bowl and leave them for at least 12 hours to plump up.

Beat the egg yolks and the sugar together until they are soft and creamy.

Heat the milk in a saucepan until it is just short of boiling point, then stir it, a little at a time, into the egg mix. Very quickly wash up the pan and dry it before putting the milk and egg mixture back into it. (This helps prevent the custard sticking to the bottom of the pan.) Over a very low heat, stir continuously until the mixture has thickened into a medium custard. Don't take your attention off it, or it may separate. Set this custard aside to cool.

Beat the spices into the pumpkin purée. When the custard is cool, stir in the pumpkin .

Whisk the cream to the soft peaks stage. Fold it into the custard mix, then stir in the raisins and any remaining rum.

If you have an ice-cream machine, put the mixture in and let the machine get on with it. Otherwise, spread the mixture evenly in a wide flat dish (I use a small baking tray) and put it in the freezer. Leave it for about 3 hours, then take it out and beat it with a fork to break up the ice crystals and soften it up, then put it back to freeze for another 2 hours, after which you can serve it.

If you want to keep it longer, transfer it to a more appropriate container and return it to the freezer. Allow it to soften in the fridge for about 30 minutes before serving.

Sweet Dumpling yoghurt ice

Frozen yoghurts are easier and quicker to make than true ice-cream, as you do not have to keep going back to stir them while they are freezing. This version, made with the chestnutty flesh of Sweet Dumpling squash, has the interesting texture of a good Indian kulfi. If you can't get Sweet Dumpling, use Acorn or Delicata.

---

4 tablespoons yoghurt
2 tablespoons orange juice
2 teaspoons orange-flavoured liqueur - Grand Marnier
     or Cointreau
100 g (4 oz) squash purée
2 teaspoons cranberry jelly
plain flour

Set out 4 small ramekins, moulds, or medium-sized bun papers. If you use the latter, place them in small dishes or a bun-baking tray, as the weight of the contents will push them out of shape before they freeze.

Stir the orange juice into the yoghurt, a little at a time, stopping if the mixture shows signs of curdling. If this happens, sprinkle in a tiny amount of plain flour before you proceed. Then gradually add the liqueur, again watching for signs of curdling.

Now mix in the squash purée and the cranberry jelly, stirring well so that everything is thoroughly incorporated. Spoon the mixture into the containers and place them in the freezer until they are solid (about 4 hours).

Serve in their containers, or unmould them. Dip solid moulds into hot water for a moment, then run a knife round the edges before inverting them over a dish. With the bun-papers, just peel the paper off.

Frozen syllabub

The classic syllabub consists of whipped cream, sugar, lemon juice and white wine. I love them, and I've been experimenting with different versions for ages, including one that uses Elderflower syrup. When I was testing the recipe for Delicata ice cream, I found that I had a little cream left over, so I whipped it up and delved in the cupboard to see what I had to make it into syllabub. I found the squash and orange jam, delved a bit more and found a bottle of Grand Marnier, whisked it all together, then since I was in 'ice cream mode', shoved it in the freezer. It was a great success, as you'll see when you try it yourself.

120 ml (4 fl oz) whipping cream
2 tablespoons squash and orange jam (see page 100)
1 tablespoon Grand Marnier

Whip the cream to just short of the soft peaks stage, then whisk in the jam and Grand Marnier and continue whisking until it is just past soft peaks. Transfer it to a flat dish and pop it in the freezer. After an hour, give it a good stir, then freeze it for another hour or so before serving.

It will keep in the freezer for several weeks, but it is best served fairly soft.

Of course, you don't have to freeze it if you want to serve it as a syllabub.

Steamed squash and ginger pudding

Although they do take a fair while to cook, few people can resist a steamed pudding, especially when it is accompanied by a good sauce. This pudding exploits squash's natural affinity with spices, and echoes one of them - the ginger - in its sauce.

500 g (1 lb) squash purée
2 eggs, beaten
150 g (6 oz) light brown sugar
100 g (4 oz) butter, melted
1 teaspoon ground cinnamon
1 teaspoon ground ginger
1/2 teaspoon grated nutmeg
pinch salt
250 g (8 oz) self raising flour
240 ml (8 fl oz) single cream

Mix all the ingredients together into a light batter and pour it into a 23 cm (9") dish. Cover this tightly with a lid or foil, then steam it for 2 hours. Serve hot with ginger sauce.

Ginger sauce

2 teaspoons arrowroot
2 tablespoons runny honey
240 ml (8 fl oz) green ginger wine
4 lumps stem ginger, finely chopped
2 tablespoons syrup from the stem ginger jar

Dissolve the arrowroot in a little water. Stir all the other ingredients together over a low heat, then stir in the arrowroot and keep stirring until the sauce is thickened.

Pumpkin wine

Having heard stories of being able to make a lethal rum-like drink by packing the seed-cavity of a ripe marrow with demerara sugar, then making a tiny hole in the end and hanging it up in an old stocking to drip into a bowl, I wondered if you could make, if not this terrifying sounding concoction, at least a wine with pumpkin. I enquired, and was told that you can make wine with anything (anything? - the mind boggles) so I tried it. I don't think the result will make the French wine-makers fear for their livings, but it does make a pleasant drink.

---

3 kilos (6 lbs) pumpkin flesh
a piece of ginger root about 5cm (2") long
4 litres (8 pints) water
1½ kilos (3 lbs) granulated sugar
3 teaspoons dried active or 'easy blend' yeast
juice of 3 lemons

This quantity makes 6 or 7 bottles.

Peel the pumpkin and cut it into chunks. Crush the ginger root with a rolling pin. Put the pumpkin and ginger in a clean bucket with 2 litres (4 pints) of the water.

Bring the rest of the water to the boil and add it to the bucket with the sugar, yeast and lemon juice. Cover the bucket with a clean tea-towel and leave it in a cool dry place to ferment for 5 - 7 days. Stir it daily.

Strain the liquid into fermentation jars with air-locks and leave it to ferment. When the fermentation has stopped and the liquid is clear, rack it off into bottles. Store the wine for at least 6 months.

Steamed baby squash with nasturtium butter (p143)

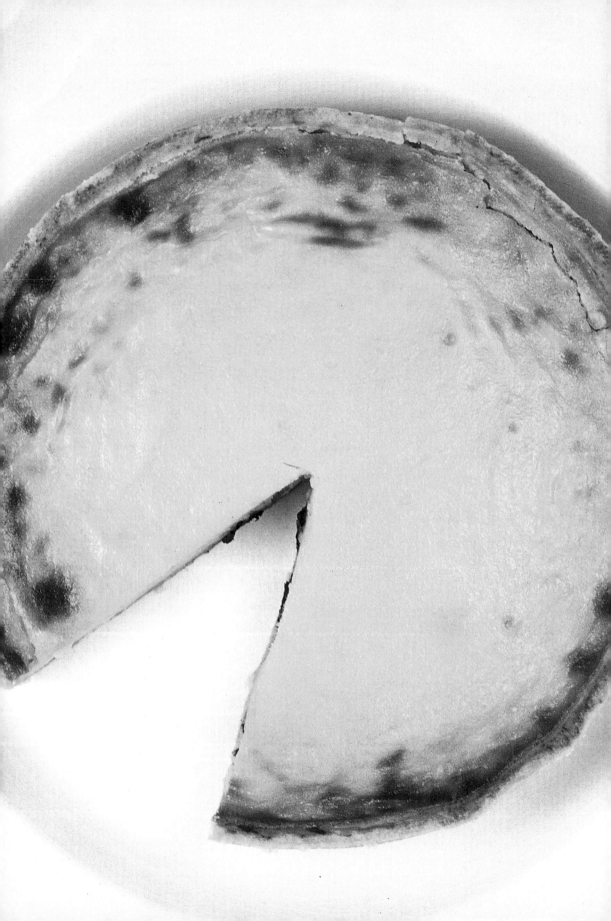

Summer squash and courgette recipes

Crispy courgettes, Neapolitan style

This is a wonderful way of preparing courgettes for an elegant starter, or pre-dinner nibbles. For a pretty dual-colour effect, use a mixture of green and gold courgettes, Pattypan squash, or even very young winter squash, if you grow them yourself. But beware - hide them away from the family until you are ready to serve them, or they will all mysteriously disappear.

---

6 large courgettes
enough olive oil to give a 10cm (4") layer in a large pan
4 tablespoons balsamic vinegar
2 cloves garlic, finely chopped
6 - 8 sprigs fresh mint, chopped
coarse sea salt

Slice the courgettes lengthwise into thin slices. Spread them out on a large tray or wooden chopping board, cover them with a clean tea-towel, and put them out in the sun for several hours to dry. Alternatively, spread them on baking trays and dry them in a very cool oven for about an hour.

Heat the oil and fry the courgette slices, a few at a time, until they are golden brown. Drain them on plenty of kitchen paper.

When all are cooked, put them in a flat serving dish and sprinkle them first with the balsamic vinegar, then with the garlic and mint, finally with the salt. Leave them to absorb the flavours for 3 or 4 hours in a cool place before serving.

Pumpkin and prune tart (p112)

Courgettes and pasta with lemon sauce

Although the idea of combining courgettes with pasta and a lemon sauce sounds odd at first, it actually works very well. The second time I tested this recipe, I didn't have enough courgettes, so I used some baby Delicata squash. The difference was barely noticeable. Don't be tempted to omit the flour - it's essential to stop the cream curdling.

6 small courgettes
500g (1 lb) pasta - ideally conchiglie or twists,
 but spaghetti will do if that's all you have handy

Lemon Sauce

100g (4 oz) butter
3 spring onions, chopped
1 teaspoon plain flour
juice of 1 lemon
250 ml (8 fl oz) single cream or 100 g (4 oz) Mascarpone
 or other cream cheese
1 tablespoon water
50 g (2 oz) Parmesan cheese, grated
1 teaspoon sugar

Cut the courgettes in half lengthways, then slice them thinly. Steam them for 4-5 minutes, until they are barely tender. Set them aside in a colander to drain off any excess water.

Cook the pasta in plenty of boiling salted water. Drain.

Meanwhile, in a separate saucepan, melt the butter and gently sauté the onions until they are translucent, but not brown. Stir in the flour, then gradually stir in the lemon juice, then the cream or cream cheese and finally half of the Parmesan. Stir in the sugar. If necessary, add a little water to adjust the texture. Taste and add salt if you feel it needs it.

When the courgettes and pasta are cooked and drained, add them to the sauce and toss the whole gently to mix. Turn it out into a dish and serve with a crisp salad and more Parmesan for diners to sprinkle on top.

Minted courgette soup

I invented this soup one hot summer day when I'd come back from our allotment with a bag full of courgettes and the first of the carrots and onions, and wanted something light for supper. A quick raid on the old sink full of mint by the back door, a delve in the fridge, and a glass of wine later we were ready to eat out on the patio where we could listen to the house-martins above us as they gathered their own supper on the wing.

---

50 g (2 oz) butter or 2 tablespoons olive oil
750 g (1 ½ lbs) courgettes, finely sliced or grated
1 medium onion, finely sliced
250 g (8 oz) carrots, finely sliced or grated
600 ml (1 pint) chicken or vegetable stock
salt
black pepper
crème fraîche for serving
6-8 fresh mint leaves, shredded

Melt the butter or oil and cook the vegetables over a gentle heat with the lid on the pan, to sweat them, for 5 - 10 minutes. Check them every couple of minutes, and if they look as though they might stick, add a ladleful of stock.

When they are just tender, liquidize them, then put them back in the saucepan with the rest of the stock. Bring the soup back to the boil then turn down the heat, season it and simmer it for 5 minutes.

Serve with a dollop of crème fraîche and a sprinkle of mint in each bowl.

Optional variation

- replace the mint with fresh dill, coriander or basil.

- for dinner parties, make two separate versions of this soup, each with a different herb, and one batch with gold courgettes or Pattypans. To serve, carefully pour a ladleful of each soup into opposite sides of each bowl so that the colours stay separate, then draw a skewer through the join to make a pattern.

Curried courgette soup

My first reaction to the suggestion of adding curry powder to courgettes was that the curry would drown the delicate flavour of the courgettes. But I was persuaded to try it, and after a couple of experiments found that it does work provided you use a very mild curry powder. If you can find some early leeks, use them, otherwise use spring onions. The best garnish for this soup is nasturtium flowers.

2 small leeks or a bunch of spring onions, finely chopped
2 tablespoons melted butter
2 teaspoons korma curry powder
1/4 teaspoon white pepper
1 kilo (2 lbs) courgettes, finely chopped
450 ml (15 fl oz) chicken stock
4 nasturtium flowers

Fry the leeks or onions in the butter until they are translucent, then stir in the curry powder and pepper. Cook for 2 minutes.

Meanwhile, bring the stock to the boil then add the onion mixture and the courgettes and simmer until they are tender. Liquidize before serving, floating a nasturtium flower on each portion.

Courgette and corn chowder

This is a thick creamy soup, garnished with crumbled crispy bacon. It's ideal for those chilly evenings which sometimes come in mid-summer, when you want something a little more filling than the usual summer soups, but don't want to go as far as resorting to winter fare.

6 slices of streaky bacon
1 small onion, finely chopped
1 small red pepper, finely chopped
6 courgettes, chopped
300 g (12 oz) sweetcorn
120 ml (4 fl oz) water
150 ml (5 fl oz) milk
150 ml (5 fl oz) single cream
1 teaspoon Worcester sauce
salt

Fry the bacon until it is crisp, then drain it, retaining the fat in the pan. Use this to fry the onion and pepper until they are soft. Add the courgettes and fry them for 2 minutes, then add the corn and water. Bring to the boil and simmer for 10 minutes, until the courgettes are tender.

Add the milk and the cream, and heat through, stirring gently. Taste and add salt if you feel the need.

Serve with a few drops of Worcester sauce and some crumbled bacon in each bowl.

Optional variation

● for a more substantial soup, add 1 fillet of smoked trout, flaked.

Steamed baby squash with choice of dressings

Serves 8

This is a delightful starter for an informal summer dinner party, where you can serve a big dish of hot, steamed baby squash with a variety of dressings to pass round. The more varied the squash you have, the better, so look for baby Pattypans in pale and dark green as well as yellow, tiny green and gold courgettes, and if you grow your own, baby winter squashes. If you can't get tiny specimens, get larger ones and quarter them - but whole babies are best.

1 kilo (2 lbs) baby squash, steamed until barely tender

Olive oil dressing - mix together

**2 - 3 tablespoons good olive oil
juice of $1/2$ lemon
$1/2$ teaspoon light brown sugar
pinch salt**

Nasturtium butter - beat together

**100 g (4 oz) unsalted butter, softened, and
1 teaspoon white wine vinegar, - then mix in
1 shallot, finely chopped
4 tablespoons chopped nasturtium flowers**

Garlic mayonnaise - mix together

4 tablespoons good mayonnaise
1 clove garlic, crushed or very finely chopped

Walnut oil and maple syrup dressing - mix together

4 tablespoons walnut oil
juice of $1/2$ lemon
2 tablespoons real maple syrup

Feta and herb dressing - liquidize together

4 tablespoons olive oil
50 g (2 oz) Feta cheese
1 tablespoon fresh thyme, basil or chives

Cream and toasted almonds -mix together

4 tablespoons single cream
50 g (2 oz) toasted flaked almonds

Courgette salads

It never occurs to most people that courgettes are delicious eaten raw. They have a crisp nutty flavour, and can be added to any combination of green salad leaves, or served in the combinations below. The smaller and fresher the courgettes, the better they taste, and in a salad, other baby squash will serve as well as actual courgettes. Slice them thinly in rondels or longitudinal sections.

Courgette and fennel salad

4 medium sized courgettes, or equivalent smaller specimens
1 bulb fennel
100 g (4 oz) green beans, lightly steamed and cooled
50 g (2 oz) green olives
dressing of 150 ml (5 fl oz) sour cream mixed
    with 1 teaspoon coarse grain mustard

Courgette and apple salad

**4 medium sized courgettes, or equivalent
    smaller specimens
2 crisp green apples, such as Granny Smiths,
    unpeeled but cored and chopped
1 red onion, chopped
1 small green pepper, chopped
dressing of vinaigrette**

Courgette and spring onion salad with pine nuts and raisins

**4 medium sized courgettes, or equivalent smaller specimens
4 spring onions, chopped
2 tablespoons pine nuts
2 tablespoons raisins
dressing of olive oil and lemon juice
2 teaspoons chopped fresh mint to sprinkle on top**

Courgette 'caviar'

**4 medium sized courgettes, or equivalent smaller specimens
    finely chopped
2 spring onions, chopped
2 cloves garlic, finely chopped
100 g (4 oz) black olives, chopped
4 leaves fresh mint, chopped
2 leaves fresh basil, chopped
1 stalk parsley, chopped
1 pinch fresh thyme**

Mix all the ingredients together, then top with 150 ml (5 fl oz) crème fraîche.

Courgette tips

In northern Italy, as autumn approaches, these 'cime di zucchini' appear in the markets, harvested by thrifty growers at the stage when the plant has stopped production at the onset of cool weather. Elsewhere you can only get them if you grow your own squash. Any squash plant will do, but courgettes are best, as they produce a good tip with a generous bunch of tiny fruits and leaves. If you don't grow your own, perhaps you could persuade your local Pick Your Own farm to let you raid their courgette patch?

You can serve them lightly steamed as a side dish, or use them to top bruschetta.

---

8 - 12 courgette plant tips, about 10cm (4") long
2 - 3 cloves garlic, finely chopped
2 - 3 tablespoons olive oil
salt
pepper
4 slices toasted bread

Steam the courgette tips for 5 minutes, until they are tender, then remove the steamer from the heat so that any excess moisture drains and evaporates. Chop them roughly.

Fry the garlic in the oil over a low heat for a couple of minutes, then turn up the heat a little and add the courgette tips. Cook for a further 2 or 3 minutes, season, and turn them out of the pan onto the slices of toast.

Simple courgette gratin

Simple in taste as well as preparation, this basic gratin is a good lunch or supper dish for those days when you don't want anything too heavy. If you want a more complex taste, you can ring the changes by using different flavoured oils, or adding some spices to the crème fraîche. If you want something a bit more substantial, you can add bread-crumbs or beaten eggs to the dish.

---

4 medium sized courgettes, thickly sliced
2 teaspoons garlic oil (see page 163)
4 tablespoons crème fraîche or thick yoghurt
100 g (4 oz) Gruyère cheese, grated

Preheat the oven to 325°F (160°C) Gas Mark 3 and butter an oven-proof dish.

Cut the courgettes into thick slices and blanch them in boiling water for 3 minutes. Drain well then lay them in the bottom of the dish.

Drizzle the garlic oil over them. Break up the crème fraîche a little with a fork and spread it over the courgettes. Sprinkle the grated cheese over the top and bake it for 15 minutes, or until the cheese has melted and is turning golden-brown.

Serve with good bread.

Optional variations

- use one of the other herb-flavoured oils instead of garlic oil.
- grate nutmeg generously over the top before baking.
- crumble a thick slice of white bread to fine crumbs and mix this with the cheese.
- beat 1 teaspoon of mild curry powder into the crème fraîche.

Provencal tian of courgette and tomato

'Tian' is the name of a flat ceramic baking dish used in Provence, which has also come to be used as a generic name for food baked in these dishes. If you don't have an authentic tian, it doesn't matter, as long as the dish you use is wide and shallow.

This has to be one of the easiest dishes to prepare, and one which retains all the flavours of the ingredients. Incidentally, my definition of large basil leaves is those enormous leaves from 'Lettuce' basil; and of small leaves those from the ordinary variety of basil, not the tiny leaves from Greek or Bush basil.

---

plain olive oil to grease the dish
2 - 3 medium sized courgettes, thickly sliced
6 - 8 ripe plum tomatoes, thickly sliced
6 large or 12 small basil leaves
50 g (2 oz) Gruyère or Parmesan cheese, finely grated
2 tablespoons garlic oil (see page 163)
coarse sea salt
pepper

Preheat the oven to 350°F (180°C) Gas Mark 4 and grease your tian.

Arrange the courgettes and tomatoes in the dish, overlapping and using courgette and tomato slices alternately.

Cut the basil into thin strips and sprinkle these on top , then sprinkle the cheese on top of that. Drizzle the garlic oil over the whole, add generous quantities of salt and black pepper, then bake for 20 minutes.

Summer squash and rice gratin

This recipe originates from America, where they would use Crookneck squash. If you can't find them, substitute young Pattypans or even courgettes. The end product will be slightly different in taste, but still delicious.

---

2 tablespoons olive oil
500 g (1lb) squash, chopped
2 spring onions, chopped
150 g (6 oz) cooked white rice
1 teaspoon dried oregano
350 ml (12 fl oz) white sauce
nutmeg

Preheat the oven to 375°F (190°C) Gas Mark 5 and butter a gratin dish.

Cook the squash and onion in the oil for 5 minutes. Mix the vegetables with the rice and spoon this mixture into a gratin dish. Sprinkle the oregano on top.

Pour the white sauce on top, and grate some fresh nutmeg over it, then bake for 25 minutes.

Optional variations

- add 100 g (4 oz) chopped cooked spinach to the courgette and rice mixture.
- add 100 g (4 oz) Ricotta cheese to the white sauce.
- Sprinkle 25 g (1 oz) flaked almonds over the top halfway through the baking time.

Courgettes as a side dish

The first courgettes of the season don't need anything other than light steaming to make them the perfect accompaniment to almost any hot meal. But as the season progresses, and especially if you grow your own and have a glut to deal with, you need to do something to stop the family moaning "Oh no, not courgettes again". So here are some ways you can perk them up a little.

Nutty courgettes

---

50 g (2 oz) butter
1 clove garlic, crushed
4 medium courgettes, sliced
50 g (2 oz) walnuts, chopped
black pepper

Melt the butter over a low heat and fry the garlic for 1 - 2 minutes. Add the cougettes and fry, stirring at intervals, for 10 minutes. Add the walnuts and a generous grinding of pepper and continue to cook, stirring, for 5 minutes.

Courgettes and peas with coriander

100 g (4 oz) butter
2 small onions, sliced
1 clove garlic, crushed
3cm (1") ginger root, grated
2 tablespoons chopped coriander leaf
4 medium courgettes, sliced
250 g (8 oz) freshly shelled peas
pepper

Melt the butter over a low heat and fry the onions and garlic for 1 - 2 minutes. Add the ginger root and coriander and fry another 2 minutes. Finally add the courgettes and peas, give the pan a good shake to mix everything well, cover the pan and cook, stirring at intervals, for 10 minutes. Serve with a generous grinding of pepper.

Garlicky courgettes (or Pattypans)

3 tablespoons olive oil
50 g (2 oz) butter
4 - 6 cloves garlic, crushed
1 kilo (2 lbs) young courgettes or Pattypans, sliced
2 tablespoons chopped parsley

Melt together the oil and butter and fry the garlic for 1 - 2 minutes. Add the courgettes and parsley and cook, covered, over a low heat, for 10 - 15 minutes, until the courgettes are tender.

Courgettes with button mushrooms

500 g (1 lb) small courgettes
500 g (1 lb) small button mushrooms
50 g (2 oz) butter
60 ml (2 fl oz) sour cream
chopped basil to garnish

Cut the courgettes into chunks the same size as the mushrooms.

Melt the butter and toss the mushrooms and courgettes in it to coat them, then turn the heat down and cook, covered, for 10 minutes until both are tender. Check them at intervals to make sure they aren't sticking. Stir in the sour cream and cook until it has warmed through before sprinkling on the basil and serving.

Herbed courgette roll-ups

This is an attractive way to present courgettes for a formal dinner, or even a buffet. Presented this way, courgettes almost become finger-food. Choose fairly large specimens, but try to avoid the ones with obvious seeds in the middle, as these won't hold together properly. For maximum visual effect, use equal quantities of green and gold courgettes.

---

butter or oil to grease the dish
3 or 4 medium to large courgettes, all the same length
100 g (4 oz) walnut pieces
1 - 2 cloves garlic, crushed
2 tablespoons chopped parsley
3 tablespoons Parmesan cheese, grated
wooden toothpicks

Preheat the oven to 425°F (220°C) Gas Mark 7 and grease a gratin dish.

Trim the ends off the courgettes, then cut them longitudinally into slices about 3mm ($^1/8$") thick. Blanch these very briefly in boiling water for just long enough to make them sufficiently pliable to roll up. Drain and separate the slices.

Purée the walnuts, garlic, parsley and two-thirds of the cheese in a blender. Spread the purée along the courgette slices and roll them up, fastening each one with a toothpick.

Stand them in the gratin dish, sprinkle the rest of the cheese on top of them and bake for about 5 minutes, until the cheese has melted and browned and they are hot right through.

Courgette fritters

Everyone is familiar with the battered and fried courgettes served in Italian restaurants. But when you try to make this dish at home, the result can be disappointing. These fritters are the solution to that problem, as they are much easier to control in the pan, and tastier too, with added ingredients to bring out all the flavour. Don't be tempted to add salt to the mixture though, as it can make the courgettes exude water, and your batter will get diluted before you've finished cooking.

---

500 g (1 lb) young courgettes, coarsely grated
1 small shallot, finely chopped
3 tablespoons plain flour
1 egg, beaten
1 tablespoon finely chopped basil, or 2 teaspoons pesto sauce
50 g (2 oz) Parmesan cheese, grated
black pepper
pinch nutmeg
olive oil for frying
balsamic vinegar (optional)

Mix all the ingredients together. Heat the oil and drop tablespoonfuls of the mixture into the pan, flattening them a little with a spatula. Depending on the size of your pan, you will be able to cook 3 or 4 fritters at once.

After about 2 minutes, lift them gently to see if the underside is golden-brown and crispy, and if it is, turn them carefully to cook the other side for another 2 minutes. Drain well on kitchen paper. Serve hot, either as they are or with a little balsamic vinegar sprinkled over them.

Optional variation

- replace the flour with fine breadcrumbs, form the mixture into walnut-sized balls, and deep fry these for 3 - 4 minutes, until golden-brown.

Golden courgette and corn purée

Purée is a misnomer for this dish, because the courgette is grated rather than puréed, but the result is a soft amalgam of tender vegetables which makes an excellent accompaniment for simple meat dishes or grilled fish. If you can't get golden courgettes don't worry too much - your dish will have flecks of green in it, but the taste will be the same.

---

4 medium golden courgettes or Crookneck summer squash,
   coarsely grated
400g tin sweetcorn
120 ml (4 fl oz) chicken or fish stock
salt
white pepper
250 ml (8 fl oz) double cream
1 tablespoon chopped chives

Put grated courgettes into a saucepan with sweetcorn and stock. Bring to the boil and simmer until the courgette is tender and all the liquid has evaporated - about 10 minutes.

Taste and season. Add the cream and cook for 5 minutes, stirring, until the cream has thickened. Serve with the chives sprinkled on top.

Crookneck soufflé

This is my version of a classic dish from Georgia (U.S.A.), which makes a good light supper dish. The original calls for the squash to be cooked very soft and then mashed, but I find that makes the soufflé rather too wet for a satisfactory rise, so I just grate the squash and blanch it lightly before proceeding. If you can't get Crookneck squash, courgettes make a perfectly good substitute.

butter to grease the dish
4 medium Crookneck squash or courgettes
2 large eggs
250 ml (8 fl oz) whipping cream
salt
white pepper
50 g (2 oz) Gruyère cheese, grated

Preheat the oven to 350°F (180°C) Gas Mark 4. Grease a deep gratin dish or 3 pint soufflé dish.

Grate the squash and blanch in boiling water for 1 minute. Drain well and let it cool.

Separate the eggs and beat the whites to the soft peak stage. In a clean bowl, whip the cream to the same stage.

Season the squash and mix the egg yolks and half of the cheese into it, then fold in the cream and egg-white. Tip the mixture into the dish and sprinkle the rest of the cheese on top. Bake for 25 minutes. Serve straightaway.

Stuffed Pattypan squash

This is what you do with the Pattypans that have grown too big to serve on their own as a side dish. By the time they are over 7cm (3") across, although the flesh is still tender, they are beginning to form seeds which are not so nice to eat. So, hollow them out and use one of these stuffings to fill the space. And of course, if you don't grow your own Pattypans, you can always use courgettes.

A variety of different coloured squash makes for a prettier dish.

Cold fillings
steam the squash lightly before filling them with one of the following:

prawns and mayonnaise
chopped spring onion, cream cheese and herbs
smoked salmon and crème fraîche
finely chopped tomato and chopped basil

Hot fillings

(The simplest of these is to use the hollow squash to serve other vegetables, such as tiny peas, pearl onions, chopped carrots or sweetcorn, either with or without a sauce.) Or try:

> **Feta cheese and herbs (parsley, tarragon and spring
>   onion or garlic chives)**
> **Caerphilly cheese and green beans**
> **quiche mixture**
> **rice, garlic and chopped mushrooms**
> **chopped tomato topped with mixed breadcrumbs
>   and grated cheese and sage**
> **mixed white and wild rice**
> **spinach, Gruyère cheese and wild mushrooms**

In each case, bake for 20 minutes at 350°F (180°C) Gas Mark 4.

Courgette and basil tarts

You can either make these as small tarts or as individual quiches. Alternatively, ring the changes in the way you arrange the courgettes, putting slices or rondels arranged on their sides so that they show the green skin against the gold of the egg custard.

> **1 recipe shortcrust pastry (page 164)**
> **5 - 6 small courgettes, sliced**
> **2 eggs**
> **150 ml (5 fl oz) single cream**
> **salt**
> **black pepper**
> **50 g (2 oz) Gruyère cheese, grated**
> **5 - 6 leaves fresh basil, shredded**

Preheat the oven to 400°F (200°C) Gas Mark 6.

Prepare the tart bases by laying the pastry in suitable baking tins. Arrange the courgettes in the pastry cases.

Beat the eggs and cream together, then mix in the grated cheese and shredded basil. Season to taste. Pour the mixture into the pastry cases, taking care not to disarrange the courgettes.

Brush the exposed pastry with milk or egg-yolk. Bake the tarts for 8 - 10 minutes, until the pastry is golden-brown and the contents are cooked. Serve hot or cold.

Herbed courgette roll-ups (p150)

Courgette 'loaf'

Although loaf-shaped, this is more of a cake as the recipe calls for baking powder and bicarbonate of soda rather than yeast. Don't be surprised if the batter seems rather sloppy - it's meant to be, and this doesn't affect the end product. It is quite rich, so serve it in small quantities, either at tea-time or with morning coffee.

---

butter to grease the tins
250 g (8 oz) golden syrup
375 g (12 oz) sunflower or corn oil
250 g (8 oz) plain flour
2 teaspoons bicarbonate of soda
1 teaspoon baking powder
1 teaspoon salt
1 teaspoon ground cinnamon
1 teaspoon grated nutmeg
3 eggs, beaten
6 - 8 drops vanilla essence
250 g (8 oz) grated courgette
250 g (8 oz) sultanas

Preheat the oven to 350°F (180°C) Gas Mark 4. Grease either 1 large or 2 small loaf tins.

Put the golden syrup and oil in a saucepan and heat them gently until the syrup has melted. Sift together the flour, bicarbonate of soda, baking powder, salt and spices.

Add the eggs to the dry ingredients and stir in the oil and syrup mixture. Finally gently fold in the grated courgettes and sultanas before pouring the batter into the loaf tins.

Bake - 75 minutes for 1 large tin, 60 for 2 smaller tins - until a skewer inserted gently into the loaves comes out clean. Take the loaves out of the oven and let them cool for 10 minutes in their tins before turning them out onto a wire rack to cool completely.

Courgette and cucumber mousse (p159)

Squash blossoms

These are a delicacy available only to those who have access to growing courgettes, squash or pumpkins, or who are lucky enough to live in a big city where such things are available in specialist shops, because they wither and start to rot within hours of being removed from the plant.

You need to know the difference between male flowers, which have long thin stems, and female flowers, which have short stems and an obvious tiny fruit behind them. Both are edible, but if you remove too many of the female flowers, you won't get any fruit. However, if weather conditions are favourable, the flower may still be usable when the fruit has grown to a couple of inches long, and you can then cut the fruit and use it with the flower attached.

Chop the petals and add them to scrambled eggs or omelettes, or sprinkle them on top of chicken soup.

Alternatively, use them stuffed with one of the fillings shown below, then battered and deep-fried. Before stuffing each flower, remove the stamen, then fill to halfway and twist the top of the petals to make a little parcel.

Rice stuffing for squash blossoms

100 g (4 oz) onion, finely chopped
1 clove garlic, crushed
2 tablespoons olive oil
250 g (8 oz) cooked rice
2 teaspoons tomato purée
2 teaspoons chopped fresh herbs (mint, basil or parsley)
salt
black pepper

Fry the onion and garlic in the oil until they are just starting to brown and stir in the other ingredients before using to stuff the flowers.

Cheese stuffing for squash blossoms

250 g (8 oz) cheese - dry cottage cheese,
    crumbled Caerphilly, or Ricotta
2 tablespoons chopped chives
50 g (2 oz) pine nuts
50 g (2 oz) raisins
salt
black pepper

Mix all the ingredients well before using to stuff the flowers.

Fettucine with sugar peas, mint and pumpkin seeds

Served with a light creamy sauce, this dish offer two contrasts - green and white colours, combined with the textural contrast of soft pasta and crunchy pea-pods and pumpkin seeds.

---

250 g (8 oz) each of green and white fettucine
100 g (4 oz) Mascarpone or cream cheese
100 g (4 oz) mangetout or sugar peas
50 g (2 oz) pumpkin seeds
1 tablespoon chopped mint leaves
grated Parmesan cheese, to serve

Cook the two colours of fettucine in separate saucepans, then drain, retaining the cooking water. Lightly steam the sugar peas.

In a large saucepan, combine the cream cheese with enough of the pasta water to make a medium thin sauce, and warm this through. Tip in the drained pasta and shake it well over a gentle heat to coat it with the sauce and warm it through. Add the sugar peas and shake again to coat them with the sauce. Finally add the pumpkin seeds and mint and shake again before serving with the Parmesan cheese.

Mexican pumpkin seed sauce

This is a hot and herby green sauce with an interesting grainy texture, served in Mexico with grilled chicken or fish. I've given you a medium hot version, but of course you can make it hotter by using more chillies. Real masochists could make it even hotter by using Scotch Bonnet peppers!

---

250 g (8 oz) pumpkin seeds
2 - 3 fresh green chillies, deseeded and coarsely chopped
leaves from a big bunch of parsley
leaves from a small bunch of coriander
generous pinch ground cumin
1/2 teaspoon ground cinnamon
pinch ground cloves
4 spring onions, chopped
2 cloves garlic, chopped
3 tablespoons corn oil
300 ml (10 fl oz) chicken or fish stock
salt

Put everything except the stock and salt in a blender and whizz it to a smooth paste. Transfer the paste to a saucepan with the stock, bring it up to the boil and simmer, stirring, until it has thickened to a sauce texture. Taste and season before serving hot or cold.

Courgette and cucumber mousse

Some years ago, a friend served a light cucumber mousse as a starter at a dinner party. Afterwards, I started experimenting, adding courgette and some other flavours, finally arriving at the version below. You can use a decorative mould and turn it out for an impressive dinner party dish, put it into ramekins, or put it in a large dish and serve slices. Eat it with good brown bread for a light lunch, or with cold chicken or salmon - and a glass of cold white wine.

The herbs could be a mixture of basil, chives, mint, parsley, tarragon, thyme or just one of these. If you include the nasturtium flowers, use a variety of colours for the most decorative effect.

½ cucumber, diced small
salt
500 g (8 oz) cottage cheese
150 ml (5 fl oz) single cream
150 ml (5 fl oz) yoghurt
1 medium or 2 small courgettes, diced small
2 - 3 spring onions, chopped small
1 tablespoon finely chopped fresh herbs
6 nasturtium flowers, chopped (optional)
1 packet jelly - lemon, lime or pineapple flavour,
    or a mixture of these (or sachet of gelatine)
2 tablespoons white wine vinegar
2 - 3 tablespoons water

Sprinkle the salt over the diced cucumber and leave it to degorge for an hour. Rinse it well, drain well, then lay it on one half of a clean tea-towel and pat it with the other half to get it as dry as you can.

Sieve the cottage cheese, or whizz it in a food processor to reduce the size of the lumps a little. Mix the cream and yoghurt together and then the cheese. Mix in the cucumber, courgette, onions, herbs and nasturtium flowers.

Melt the jelly in the vinegar and water, using as little water as possible. Let this stand for a moment to take the heat off it, then pour it into the main mixture, stirring well. Pour it into selected containers, and put it in the refrigerator to set and chill.

Tip

• use gelatine rather than jelly if you prefer a less sweet mixture.

Courgette omelette

I originally encountered this dish as cucumber omelette. It's fine in that form, but just as I prefer my omelettes to be fairly well done, so I prefer the denser flesh and nuttier taste of courgettes as a filling.

---

2 medium courgettes, grated or finely chopped
50 g (2 oz) butter
2 tablespoons thick yoghurt
1 tablespoon chopped mint (optional)
8 eggs
salt
pepper
butter to grease the pan

Cook the courgettes gently in the butter for 4 - 5 minutes. Take them off the heat and stir in the yoghurt and mint.

For each person, beat 2 eggs with a little salt and pepper. Heat the omelette pan, grease it with a little butter, pour in the eggs and let them cook until the underneath is firm and the top is set to your taste. Spoon a quarter of the courgette mixture down one half and fold the other half over it before turning it out of the pan.

Optional variation

● add a little chopped ham and replace the mint with parsley.

Cucumber, mint and cider sorbet

This is a delightful sorbet, combining the coolness of cucumber with the tang of mint and an added piquancy from the cider. I had thought, when the idea came to me, that it would make a good 'mouth-freshener' between courses for a summer dinner, but I ended up adding a little more sugar to it and making it sweet enough for a dessert.

Like most sorbets, it contains egg-white, which helps to keep it frozen, but you can omit this if you wish, as long as you are able to serve it quickly, as sorbet without egg-white melts very quickly.

---

1 large cucumber
100 g (4 oz) caster sugar
juice of 1/2 lemon
4 - 6 tablespoons sweet cider
1 tablespoon finely chopped mint
white of 1 egg

Peel the cucumber and chop it roughly, then liquidize it in a food processor or liquidizer. Put the sugar into a bowl, put a strainer over the top of the bowl and pour the liquidized cucumber into the strainer so that it drips onto the sugar. Leave it to drip for an hour or so.

Press the last of the juice out of the cucumber but don't push any of the flesh through the sieve. Dispose of the cucumber pulp, or use it to make cucumber and courgette mousse (see page 159).

Add the lemon juice and stir the liquid until the sugar has dissolved. Add the cider, tasting to see if you feel the whole 6 spoonsful should be used. Stir in the chopped mint.

If you have an ice-cream machine, put the mixture in and let the machine get on with it. Otherwise, spread the mixture evenly in a wide flat dish (I use a small baking tray) and put it in the freezer. Leave it for about 2 hours, then whisk the egg white to the soft peaks stage. If using a machine, add the egg white to the mixture in the machine and let it work for another 15 - 20 minutes. If using a tray in the freezer, beat the sorbet with a fork to break up the ice crystals and soften it up, then beat in the egg white and put it back to freeze for another hour, after which you can serve it.

• This dish contains uncooked eggs, and thus should not be given to the very young, the very old, the ill, pregnant women, or anyone else likely to be vulnerable to salmonella.

Courgette chocolate cake

In America, people suffer from such gluts of courgettes that they have devised various techniques to get rid of them, including sneaking out late at night to put them in unsuspecting householders' mailboxes. Some of the recipes that have grown from this situation include breads and cakes, where grated courgette retains the moisture in the same way that carrot does in carrot cake. It's so effective that this courgette chocolate cake has become a classic, and every cook has their own version. This one uses cocoa powder and chocolate chips, giving a double dose for chocoholics.

100 g (4 oz) butter, softened
120 ml (4 fl oz) vegetable oil
350 g (12 oz) soft brown sugar
2 large eggs, beaten
120 ml (4 fl oz) milk
350 g (12 oz) self raising flour
4 tablespoons cocoa powder
1/2 teaspoon salt
1 teaspoon vanilla essence
500 g (1 lb) courgettes, grated
250 g (8 oz) chocolate chips (of your choice - bitter, milk
    or white chocolate)

Topping (optional)

200 g pack cream cheese, softened
500 g (1 lb) icing sugar
50 g (2 oz) walnut halves
2 - 4 teaspoons cocoa powder (optional)

Preheat the oven to 375°F (190°C) Gas Mark 5 and grease and line a deep baking pan approximately 20 by 30 cm (9 by 12").

Cream the butter, oil and sugar together until they are smooth, then gradually beat in the eggs and milk. Sift the flour and cocoa powder together and fold gently into the butter mixture.

Stir in the vanilla and salt, then fold in the grated courgettes and chocolate chips. Pour the mixture into the prepared tin and bake for 35 - 45 minutes, until firm and a skewer comes out clean. Allow to cool in the tin before cutting into squares to serve.

If you want to ice the cake, beat the cream cheese into the icing sugar with the cocoa powder. You may need a few drops of water to give a thick spreading consistency. Spread this over the cake with a palette knife, then arrange the nuts on top. Leave for a couple of hours for the icing to settle before cutting the cake.

Basic recipes

Flavoured oils

These serve a dual purpose - they are a quick and easy way to introduce flavours into dishes and can be stored throughout the winter when the flavouring element (e.g. basil or tarragon) is impossible or expensive to obtain. Use a good extra virgin olive oil, but don't waste your money by using a single estate version, as the subtle flavours of the oil will be lost when you add your chosen flavouring element. Then just put the flavouring element in a clean bottle - several sprigs of herbs, or several crushed garlic cloves or chilli peppers - and fill the bottle with oil.

Leave it for at least two weeks before using. There is no need to take the flavouring element out of the bottle before using the oil.

Elderflower syrup

Ever since I discovered elderflower syrup one hot summer, it has become one of my store cupboard essentials. Actually, I keep it in my freezer, because it has a tendency to ferment otherwise, and although that can make for some very interesting results, it's not always what I want.

---

1 litre (2 pints) water
1 kilo (2 lbs) granulated sugar
juice of 1 lemon
10 - 12 flower heads of elder (ideally still with pollen
        on the flowers)

Boil the water and add the lemon juice and the sugar. (Don't be tempted to put the lemon skin in, as this makes the syrup bitter.) Stir until the sugar has dissolved, then put in the elder flowers, push them under and continue to cook until the water has returned to the boil. Turn off the heat, cover the pan and leave to infuse for at least 12 hours.

Strain and bottle the syrup.

To make a refreshing drink, put 1 - 2 tablespoons of syrup in a glass and top it up with fizzy water.

Shortcrust pastry

If you don't want to make pastry by hand you can cheat, as I must confess I often do, by buying it ready made and rolled out to fit pie plates. For those who do want to make their own here's the basic recipe.

---

250 g (8 oz) plain flour
generous pinch salt
50 g (2 oz) butter or margarine
50 g (2 oz) lard or other white fat
4 tablespoons water
a little more flour to sprinkle on the board and rolling pin

The trick to making successful pastry is for everything to be cold. Serious pastry makers swear by a marble slab for rolling it out, but this isn't really necessary. However, if you put the flour in the fridge for an hour or so before you start, and use ice water, you'll be well on your way. Finally, if you are working by hand rather than with a food processor, wash your hands in cold water before you start.

By hand

Sift the flour and salt into a large bowl, then cut the fats into small pieces and add them to the bowl. With the tips of your fingers, or a pastry-mixing 'cutter', rub the fat into the flour until the mixture resembles fine breadcrumbs. Add the water a little at a time, and with a fork or the cutter, mix it in. Finally use your fingers to bring the whole mass into a ball and turn this out onto your rolling surface. Use a rolling pin to roll the pastry to the desired thickness.

By machine

Sift the flour and salt together, then put them into the machine. Cut the fats into small pieces and add them before running the machine until the mixture resembles fine bread-crumbs, then add the water a little at a time, with the motor still running, until the dough forms a ball. Switch the machine off and proceed as above.

Bechamel (white) sauce

I can never understand why people make such a fuss about making a simple white sauce by the classic method. It isn't difficult, if you exercise a little patience, and it's actually easier, to my mind, than the alternative of using cornflour. It tastes considerably better, too.

50 g (2 oz) butter
1 tablespoon plain flour
450 ml (³/4 pint) milk
salt
white pepper

Melt the butter in a saucepan and stir in the flour to make a roux. Then gradually add the milk, stirring constantly, until the sauce is the consistency you desire. Taste and season.

Tip

- If you are making the sauce for a savoury dish that involves onions or other vegetables, start by frying the onions in the butter, then adding the flour and milk as above.

Cheese sauce

All you have to do to make a cheese sauce is make a white sauce, then stir in enough grated cheese to give the depth of cheesiness you desire. In general, a sauce made with 450 ml (16 fl oz) of milk will need 75 to 100 g (3 to 4 oz) cheese. A teaspoon of dry mustard powder gives an added piquancy.

Raspberry or strawberry coulis

100 g (4 oz) frozen raspberries or strawberries, thawed
1 tablespoon icing sugar
1 tablespoon fruit liqueur (optional)

Whizz the fruit and sugar together in a liquidiser or food processor, then put the result through a fine sieve to get rid of the pips. Stir in the liqueur just before serving.

Useful addresses

Seed suppliers

In the UK, most seed companies offer a couple of varieties of pumpkin, and possibly also a couple of winter squash. (All offer a range of courgettes and cucumbers.) For a wider range of seeds, get the catalogues from:

Suffolk Herbs, Monks Farm, Coggleshall Road, Kelvedon, Essex. CO5 9PG Tel: 01376 572456 (Retail and wholesale);

The Henry Doubleday Research Association, Ryton Organic Gardens, Coventry CV8 3LG. Tel: 01203 303517 (Retail);

A L Tozer Ltd, Pyports, Downside Bridge Road, Cobham, Surrey KT11 3EH. Tel: 01932 862059 (Wholesale only).

Tip

- seeds of all the squashes and pumpkins will stay viable for at least six years if you keep them in a cool dry place, so why not buy a couple of different varieties each year and plant just a few of each?

French pumpkin fairs

These are the regular dates and locations of major 'manifestations' of pumpkins, squashes, gourds and other rare vegetables. All start at around 8 am and go on all day and into the evening.

Third weekend in September - 57 Rue Groison, Tours, and Saint-Brisson-sur-Loire. (Loiret); Last weekend in September - Millancay (Loir et Cher); First Sunday in October - Marchiennes (Nord); Second Sunday in October - Tranzault (Indre); Third weekend in October - Eaubonne (Val-d'Oise); First weekend in November - Saint-Remy-la-Varenne (Maine-et-Loire); Weekend closest to 11 November - Saint-Jean-de-Beauregard (Essonne).

Giant pumpkins

The UK Giant Pumpkin Championships are held each year at Baytree, near Spalding in Lincolnshire, in the middle of September. The championships are run by the British National Pumpkin Society.

Contact the secretary, Mike Turner, at

2 The Laurels,

Shepherds Lane,

Great Packington,

Meriden,

Nr Coventry CV7 7JU

Tel: 01676 523339 for full details of the competition, and for membership details. Members receive seeds from prize-winning giant pumpkins and advice on growing them.

Index of pumpkin and squash types

Index of secondary main ingredients